C000157739

Life at Lairds

- memories of working shipyard men.

by

David Roberts

"The time may not be far off when young people will ask, what did they do, what were they like, those who worked there?
This book answers the questions."

Sea Breezes

"A book full of anecdotes and rich in humanity....a piece of social history."

Liverpool Echo

An Avid Publication

Printed by
MFP Design & Print,
Longford Trading Estate,
Thomas Street, Stretford,
Manchester, M32 0JT.
Tel : 0161 864 4540 Fax: 0161 866 9866.

Other books and videos from AVID are detailed on the inside
back cover of this book.
They can be obtained direct from AVID on:
Tel / Fax (44) 0151 645 2047
or e-mail info@AvidPublications.co.uk

For my dad, John Ivor Roberts, a Lairds cranedriver for most of his life. I think he would have liked it. Also for my wife Denise with all my love. (Verbatim Transcript) and for Luke David Roberts, aged 11, my son.

Acknowledgements

My wife Denise
   Who works very hard for us all and gives me the time and the space.
Julie Brown and Pauline Dickson
   Writers themselves, for labouring over the taped transcripts of the
   contributors, the big ones and the little ones. I am eternally grateful..
Noel and Rita Kirkpatrick
   Of the City of Belfast, for their advice and guidance, and telling me to go
   for it.
Alan Cowderoy
   Lecturer in Photography at Wirral Metropolitan College.For his advice,
   technical expertise and patience.
Peter Mullane and Peter Bullock
   Photographers , who , as the two 'Ps' visited all of the contributors and
   provided portraits
Brian Ainscough
   For his technical advice
Mark Rickards
   My friend,for reading the manuscript, talking it through, and pushing me
   on when I had doubts.
John Haggerty
   Also my friend, who showed me how to beat B.T. and who was there
   when Avid arrived.
Maureen Robinson
    For the battery

   My thanks are also due to the many people, too numerous to mention.
for the loan of photographs that they have held for many years.
   Finally to the men and woman who took the time to talk to me. Especially
John Cropper, who put me in touch with many contributors, and who, along
with many of the other contributors, finished their working life in Lairds during
the final editing of this book. I wish then all good fortune for the future I know
that some of my questions brought back bad as well as good memories for some
of them. I hope I have done you justice.

David Roberts 1993

Contents

A VIEW

Captain Nemo spoke with captivating eloquence. His fiery look and passionate gestures transfigured him. Yes! He did love his vessel like a father loves his child."But how could you construct this admirable Nautilus in secret?"

" I had each separate portion made in different parts of the globe, and it reached me through a disguised address. The keel was forged at Creuzot, the shaft of the screw at Penn and Co.'s of London; the iron plates at Laird's of Liverpool; the screw itself at Scott's of Glasgow..........all of these people had my orders under different names".

From Twenty Thousand Leagues Under the Sea by Jules Verne. 1870

The above perhaps explains and illustrates three things. Firstly , the almost fanatical affiliation that men have with ships. Second, the international renown of the Laird company in the nineteenth century and finally, and I claim writers license here, Lairds 'flexibility' in the acceptance of orders,whatever their source. 'Twenty Thousand Leagues Under the Sea' was published only five years after the end of the American Civil war, a war during which Lairds accepted the contact to build the infamous raidership Alabama for the Confederate south, a blatant breach of Britains neutrality of the time.

Or, as the Conservative government and Vickers Shipbuilding and Engineering Ltd. (VSEL) would say, Business is Business.

4

The Author

I was born in Birkenhead and lived in the family home of 36 Holt Hill Tranmere until I was 21 years old. I went to Mersey Park Primary School and what was then Park High Grammar School for Boys where my blazers were supplied by the sons of Mrs Rowlands who had the corner shop at the bottom of Holt Hill. Thanks again Phil, though it didn't do me much good at the time.

On leaving school my daily routine was to walk down Holt Hill and then Green Lane every working day for five years as I served my apprenticeship as a fitter. Like many of the men in this book, I really didn't know what Lairds was all about, despite the fact that my father was working there. I remember meeting a lad called Tommy Upham, who lived around the corner from me in Helmingham Square flats. He told me he was going to be a fitter in Lairds. I asked him what a fitter did. He wasn't sure but thought it was something to do with fixing telephones. My family had just got a telephone and I thought that this was a thing for the future. I'm still waiting to fix my first telephone.

When the company was in financial trouble , again , in 1970/71, I was one of many young men who, with minimum entitlement to redundancy payments, were made redundant. Life was different then in the pre-Thatcher years and it was a simple case of deciding where you wanted to go to work for your next job.

A career in engineering followed, then a University degree. I now teach whoever will let me teach them, write and publish books, and talk about ships and the sea on local radio.

This is my second book on the subject of Cammell Laird. Shipping and shipbuilding apart my other interests are the poetry of Byron and the economic development of Japan.

Chronology

1824 Founding of Birkenhead Iron Works by William Laird at Wallasey Pool.

1828 John Laird joins the firm. Now Wm. Laird & Son. First iron ship built.... the WYE. A 90 foot lighter for the Irish Inland Steam Navigation Co.

1832 First ocean going voyage by an iron vessel ,the ALBURKAH ,taken by Macgregor Laird on his first West African Expedition.

1837 First screw driven ship the ROBERT.F.STOCKTEN.

1840 First iron ship to be owned by British Government,the DOVER.

1846 Building of the famous paddle man-of -war BIRKENHEAD for the British Government.

1852 Macgregor Laird founds African Steamship Co. Lairds build 5 steamers for this company Forerunner, Faith, Hope, Charity and Northern Light.This company was later to become the world famous Elder Dempster Company.

1856 Lloyds of London issue first specification for iron ships.

1858 Wallasey land required for development of docks and taken over by the newly formed Mersey Docks and Harbour Board. John Laird is appointed to M.D.H.B.as it's government nominee.Lairds move to new site betwen Monks Ferry and Tranmere Pool.

1861 John Laird retires from the business .Control goes to sons William, John and Henry.

1862 Launch of the ALABAMA the infamous raider for the Confederates in the American civil war.Vessel no.290, launched as the ENRICA. Paradoxically, a wooden ship.

1863 John Laird becomes first M.P. for Birkenhead.
Company now known as Laird Brothers .

1873 Death of John Laird

1900 Becomes a public company Laird Brothers and Co. Ltd.

1903 Amalgamation with Charles Cammell , a Sheffield based
Steel manufacturer. Now Cammell Laird and Co.Ltd.

1910 End of Laird family connection. Last "Laird " Chairman,
J.Macgregor Laird dies. New head of company is William
Lionel Hitchens.

1915 Lairds build first experimental submarine the E41.

1917 King George V and Queen Mary visit the yard to celebrate
output of over 150,000 tons of war shipping.

1920 Completion of first ever all welded vessel the Fullagar, for
the Anchor and Brocklebank Line.

1922 New Managing Director Mr.Robert (later Sir Robert)
Stewart Johnson, father of Robert White Johnson the
Managing Director of Lairds during "the polaris years."

1927 Completion of Her Majesty's Battleship Rodney, launched
by H.R.H. Princess Mary.

1931 Depression sees only one vessel under constuction at Lairds.
Workforce approx. 2000.

1934 Lairds builds it's 1000th ship, the 5000 ton cargo liner
CLEMENT for the Booth Steamship Co.of Liverpool.

1935 Order for the first ship to be designed and built as an
aircraft carrier, Ark Royal. Launched 2 years later and
watched by an estimated crowd of 30,00 people.

1938   Launch of the Mauritania for the Cunard Company.

1939   Loss of 99 lives when Lairds built submarine Thetis fails to
surface on sea trials off Angelsey.

1940   Robert Stewart Johnson becomes Chairman .

1939-1945 Lairds build 106 fighting ships. An average of one
every 20 days.

1951   Robert Stewart Johnson dies.His son Robert White Johnson
becomes Managing Director of the company. J.C. Mather
becomes chairman.

1954   Company now becomes Cammell Laird and Co.
(Shipbuilders and Engineers.)

1955   Completion of Lairds second Ark Royal aircraft carrier.

1959   Launch of the Windsor Castle by H.M. Queen Mother, for
Union Castle Company.

1960   Launch of first ever gas-turbine powered guided missile
destroyer Devonshire for the Admiralty.

1962   Princess Alexandra opens new Princess Dock.Then the
largest privately owned dry dock in Britain.
Amalgamation with local firm of Grayson, Rollo and Clover
shiprepairers and engineers.

1963   Award of contract ,from H.M.Government to build two
nuclear powered Polaris Submarines.

1964   Keel laid of ship no. 1316.   Polaris submarine Renown.

1965   Formation of Cammell Laird Group with subsidiaries..
Cammell Laird and Co. (Shipbuilders and Engineers) and
Cammell Laird (Shiprepairers)
Keel laid of ship no.1317 Polaris submarine Revenge.

1967 Workforce numbers almost 12,000 .
Keel laid of ship no. 1330. Hunter Killer nuclear submarine (non- polaris) Conquerer. Later to gain enormous publicity as the vessel that sank the Argentine battleship the General Belgrano in the South Atlantic during the Falklands conflict.

1968 Handover of H.M.S Renown

1969 Handover of H.M.S.Revenge

1970 Financial reconstruction of the company.H.M.Government take 50% interest in Cammell Laird & Co. (Shipbuilders and Engineers.)The shipbuilding company ceases to be a part of the Laird Group.

1972 Company now Cammell Laird Shipbuilders Ltd. Old camel logo replaced with CL monogram design. Government announces plans to financially assist Lairds modernisation programme.

1976 Completion of HMS Birmingham first of three type 42 destroyers for Royal Navy.

1977 Company nationalised as part of British Shipbuilders.

1978 Completion of modernisation progamme. New covered 145m*107m* 50m high "construction hall".

1985 Company denationalised to becomes a subsidiary of Vickers Shipbuilding and Engineering Ltd. (V.S.E.L.)

1991/2 The company workforce numbers under 2,000.Three conventional submarines of the Upholder class are under construction.The third one of these HMS UNICORN was the last vessel to be built at Cammell Lairds.

1993 After more than 170 years of shipbuilding on the River Mersey, the Birkenhead shipyard of Cammell Lairds closed down.

Introduction

The Birkenhead Shipyard of Cammell Laird and Company Ltd has been around, in one form or another since 1824. The first ship built there, the iron lighter WYE ,was completed in 1828. At the time of writing that is almost 170 years of shipbuilding history. 170 years of history that is almost certainly coming to an end because of politics, economics and competition.

The achievements of this company are so many that it is difficult to be concise in describing them. First iron ship to be owned by the British Government. First crossing of the Atlantic ocean by a screw driven vessel, first all welded ship in the world, first purpose built aircraft carrier , first gas turbine driven vessel for the Royal Navy..it is a long list and a chronology of some of these events is included in this book.

The owners of the shipyard until the early 20th century were the Laird family, who gave the town of Birkenhead its' first, second and third Member of Parliament and was largely responsible for building the town of Birkenhead around the shipyard. Roads, houses, libraries and hospitals all benefited from the Lairds family business. The graves of John Laird and other members of the family are still today in a quiet corner of the Birkenhead Priory which ironically, were it not for a four metre high wall,overlooks what is left today of this once huge enterprise.

During two world wars Cammell Laird answered the call to produce and repair the ships that were needed to feed and defend this island nation. In fact, during the second world war Cammell Laird produced a ship every 21 days!

It is ironic in the extreme that the year that commemorates the 40th anniversary of the Battle of the Atlantic, complete with sailpasts and courtesy visits to the Mersey of some of these vintage ships, should also see the demise of a shipyard that supplied innumerable vessels that took part in that titanic struggle.

This company employed more than 15,000 men at one time, today this figure is in the low hundreds and dwindling as I write. The effects of this rundown and ultimate closure are immeasurable in both a social and a manufacturing sense. Somewhere along the line just about everyone who lives within 10 miles of the shipyard has had their lives touched by Cammell Lairds. A father, brother,son, uncle or just a neighbour or friend will have worked there at some time or other.

Many will have visited the yard as schoolchildren to watch a ship being launched.

My own family was no different. My father worked at Lairds for his life as a cranedriver and managed to support a wife and six children, who are all still here to tell the tale.I can only now appreciate just how difficult a management act that was. I too went to see launches and I suppose that there was an element of inevitability, regardless of whatever education I received, that I would work in Cammell Lairds one day. I did. I served an engineering apprenticeship in Lairds in the late sixties and enjoyed every minute of it.These were the years between 16 and 21 years of age when boys change into men and this is a very impressionable time. Cammell Lairds turned out so many men from boys that the place can arguably be described as a social catalyst of its time,moulding opinions and ideas about and within an industrial society.

We all know that this is not the case in the nineties. Many of the people who lose their jobs at Cammell Lairds now may never work again, and, perhaps even more regrettably, Cammell Laird will no longer provide a training for young men as they did for me any many others.

The idea behind this book was an attempt to look at the history of the yard in a different way from my last book on Cammell Lairds. The famous ships, the pioneering innovation and the world wide fame the company enjoyed are, of course, part of what made the name of Cammell Laird. But the real shipbuilders are the ordinary men, and some women, who worked in the shipyard and built ships.

If this shipyard dies, and a last minute reprieve seems less probable by the day, then only those that worked in Lairds can ever know and understand what shipbuilding on the River Mersey was all about. Two or three generations on,our childrens children may know little of what this place was. Or that it was ever there. This book is an attempt to tell them.

But then why should anyone want to tell the story of lives spent building ships? The answer is difficult. There is something about ships that evokes deep feelings in people, more so if you have been involved in building them and sending them to sea, or sailing upon them. They are very large items, unlike motor cars or television sets, ships are individuals and are even sexed as female. Each one is different and performs different tasks upon the water, an element that men can only exert minimal control over through ships.

Perhaps it is because at base, we are, and always will, be an island race. It is approximated that in 1800 there were 300,000 seafarers in a population of 12 million, 2.5% of the population of Britain. There is a more than better possibility that somewhere in all our histories there was a mariner and this is a notion that has never been completely erased from the British psyche.

Whatever it is that makes ships special to us it is clear that something happens to people when ships, the sea, wars or disasters at sea are in our minds.

With this idea in mind I have asked Cammell Laird workers about their lives in the shipyard and their thoughts about this part of their lives coming to an end. They talked about their first days in the yard, old ships and hardships, characters and dangers, and their thoughts about the kind of epitaph that Cammell Lairds might have.

These are some of the people who experienced life at Lairds and have recorded their memories at my behest. I have tried to keep the editing to a minimum in order to try to give the reader access to actually listening to shipbuilders talking about their lives.

There are some terms that are unique to shipbuilding and to explain these in the text would, in my view, be distracting, so I have added a short glossary of some shipbuilding expressions.

The contributors are all, with one exception, men, some of whom still worked at Lairds in the spring of 1993. All of them willingly gave their permission to use their voices in this book.

They can , of course, at best, only be a cross section of shipbuilders and I have tried hard to produce a spread of the diverse trades involved in the building of a ship. I believe that they are representative, and to those many hundreds of shipyard workers whose names do not appear here, I can only hope that these voices will echo yours.

These are the voices of some of the men who built the ships that went down to the sea and carried the navies and the food, the coal and the iron, and the weapons of war. The ships that are part of the history of Britain.

What follows is what life at Lairds was like.

Jim Hancock
Aged 90

Boilermaker-Plater
Worked in Lairds
1917-1967

I didn't really know what a plater was but a friend had told me that it was a good job. I remember going down to Lairds and my father going to see Mr.Mullen the head foreman, they played in the same rugby team . He started me up but no favours. Just sent me to work for 10 shillings a week. That was in 1917. I was a marker boy at first until I was 16. A marker boy was someone who is like a helper for a Journeyman Plater, making templates and things like that.

I had a bad start on my first day on the ships,it was a submarine...I didn't like the journeyman I was with and so asked Mr. Mullen for a move. He said .... you can't pick and choose your jobs you know....but in the end he moved me and put me with Bert Cabot. During the war (1st) we worked 6.00am to 5.15pm...53 hours a week. You might be on a ship lifting templates for some job and the next you were back in the shop making them...or you might be screwing up some deckplates. The erectors erected the job then they would want them screwed up properly. You worked in the rain and go home without pay if it got too wet.

I got an extra docket for going to night school, this was

13

given by Sir George Carter...I was one of only a few apprentice platers who passed a 2 year technical course 1st Class.This meant a 2 shilling rise and a 2 shilling lump sum...a 4 shilling a week docket. This was extra on top of my wages. When the head foreman saw me getting this docket he played hell with me......what was I doing working day work, everyone was on piecework then? He wouldn't let me explain and told me to fetch my foreman. I did and the foreman said .....if he's working on a docket he must be bluffing !

Eventually the platers head foreman found out that it was true...the next thing he had me in the shop...at 18 running a squad. A squad was a plater and 4 of 5 apprentices. One lad was about 20 from Belfast...he had to get out of Belfast because he'd seen a murder or something like that. His name was Mickey Kerr. But they didn't mark off in Belfast the way we did so although he was older I ended up running the squad not him because he didn't understand it properly. When I was 19 I had 13 apprentices in my squad.

It was always Mr. then for the bosses..it was a very strict place, you couldn't have a cup of tea in the mornings or a fire by your bench in the winter. If you were late that was that, you could be in the queue at the tally offices at Green Lane 2 or 3 minutes before starting time and if the timekeeper hadn't booked us all on then the window would drop and you had to go home. I used to leave home , Redmond Street in Tranmere ,and run down the hill to book on. Then they moved the tally offices up on the slipways, which was a long way from Green Lane gate... then you had to get up there on time or the same thing would happen...window down and that was it.

In 1921 I came out of my time but had to make up 3 months lost time. I had been off sick for 3 months when I was 16 so I had to make this time up before I was out of my time.This was important to us because we would be on journeymans rates and we would get back our indenture money...that was five pounds that we had paid in at a shilling a week...that was to make sure that you behaved yourself as an apprentice, if you didn't do what's right you lost your Indentures.

Me and two of my mates used to go to Rossi's in Chester Street for an ice- cream and we said that when we came out of our time we would go the Rossi's and celebrate with half a dozen ice-creams.... I don't remember how many ice-creams we had but we did do it.

I remember the Fullagar (the first all welded sea going vessel in the world ...1920) she was named after the engine. The engine that went into it was called a Fullagar.. I was on her for a short while....We knew it was a special boat...but it was only small, about 100 feet long. I'd seen electric welders before but never on a ship. They still had to use rivets to screw the plates up , they butt weld seams these days but then they didn't know how to do that, so they were lapped joints...so each plate would have a rivet hole in every 2 feet to screw up the plates then they would weld over the rivets...I'm pretty sure they was no flux on the rods then..just the bare metal.

The Boilermakers Union was around then but not as strong...I didn't have much to do with them but they did help us...it was getting so the firm could do what they liked...they could turn round and drop my price, say I was doing a job for 5d each they could just drop that if they felt like it.

I spoilt a job once, I spoilt a plate and I was given another plate and nobody ever knew about it. We buried the other plate in the ground..there was no tarmac or anything then. Years later they came to asphalt the floor and found the plate...but we cut it up for something else before anyone saw it.

Another time I was at home worrying about the measurements on some intercostals that we had been doing. I couldn't get it out of my mind so I went back down the yard about 7.30pm,, all dressed up too I was, to see the frame squad who were working overtime. I spoke to the frame squaddie, Jimmy Robb and he checked everything out and it was OK, thank goodness.

I was laid off twice ...which wasn't much really...a 7 week and an 11 week. It did me good in a way...when I came back to work I felt more independent, I felt a man somehow. I felt I hadn't got to bow down...I can't explain the feeling but I'd got more confidence somehow. I remember starting back on the Monday morning, doing a job on deck ..No 5 hatch. There was a manager there..I'd played rugby against him and we knew each other but he never looked at me. He kicked my heel and said

" Hey you...go down and brighten those lines on the seat down in the engine room."

This was my first day back so I got up and said,

"If you asked me respectfully I would have done that."

He told my foreman and I asked the foreman

"Do you want them brightening Frank ?"

He said " If you don't mind Jim." so I went and did the job.

I wouldn't have done that once...spoken back to him like that.

I remember the Ark Royal too, both of them, but I get a bit mixed up with them...on the 2nd one you wouldn't believe how much steel could be put on a ship in such a short time....Lairds were taking anyone and anybody to get the job done...there was steel all over the yard covered in paraffin. There was a deck edge lift on the side of the ship for the aeroplanes...it was made of a special type of steel...you daren't put a scriber on it.. You couldn't scratch or dab it. They had a hell of a job marking it off.

The Mauritania too...that was built in 13 months from keel to launch..we were working all day and all night. For the tonnage it was the quickest ship ever built in the country in my opinion.

During the war (2nd) you didn't really have time to be frightened...I just remember other men quoting what they would do if the warning went off. They said they'd go home to their wives. We'd got gas masks hanging up in the shops and I remember one day three aeroplanes , which should have come up the Dee and then crossed over by Heswall coming up the Mersey instead. This was only about the 4th day of the war...they were opened fire on, but were flying low over the river. We went down our air raid shelter which was an electrical pit. All the chaps who said they'd go home to their wives didn't know what to do, they didn't take their gas masks and they all just went anywhere.

Another time there was a warning, we were working all night and we had a shelter at the end of the slipway. Three of us and a Cranedriver and a driller. We ran into the shelter. We didn't feel anything but Mason Street got it. When we came to get out the shelter had moved and we were walking in a different direction to what we had come in from.The blast must have moved the shelter but we didn't feel anything.

We all did foreigners in Lairds too. Once, the head foreman was taking something out in his car, at 9 o'clock at night. We were taking it to his car and the yard bobby came along. He just winked at us.

I made a shelter for home too. Mother had gone blind and she lived with my sister in Bebington Road and they had no shelter. It was one that just fitted under the stairs. Three people could sit in it with their backs to the width of the stairs.It was a bolt together job. I got it out on the galvanising wagon. The galvanising people didn't know about it but their driver would take it out with all the other stuff and drop it off for you.

I don't really think that you could get a better class of tradesman than was in Cammell Lairds, a lot came from other shipyards, but they weren't up to the standards of Cammell Lairds. I did 51 years in Lairds and don't have one regret, I couldn't have had a better place to suit me, nobody could have had a better working life. When I was on the multiple punch I worked my holidays for nothing. I used to think if I ever came into a lot of money , I wouldn't like to give up my job.

I think old John Laird made the town but he also brought a lot of strangers into it as well. Considering the working,it was a good firm, I enjoyed every bit of it.

Now... I don't understand, ...it upsets me... I just can't understand it.

The Fullager. Only 45 metres long, she was the first all welded sea going vessel in the world, arguably the greatest technical advance of the century in shipbuilding. Completed in 1920. Jim Hancock remembers working on her.

The first purpose built Aircraft Carrier for the Royal Navy. HMS Ark Royal circa 1938.

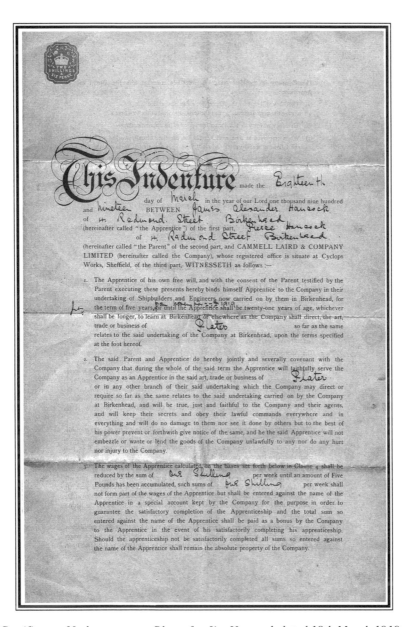

Certificate of Indentures as a Plater for Jim Hancock dated 18th March 1919

Bobby Shacklady
Aged 58

Cranedriver
Worked in Lairds
1954-1964
Now a professional
comedian

On my first day is was in the O.E.D (Outside Engineering Department. Frank Shaw sent me to see Bill Robinson (Cranedrivers Foreman) and he gave me a little ginny in the welding bay. I soon realised what sort of job it was. I was getting all the fumes and the flashes and the noise... sparks everywhere, everything was filthy..covered in oil. One of the lads showed me , told me I had to oil this and oil that with dirty clothes.

But by the end of the week I was beginning to like it. I cleaned out the cabin, got it to my own liking and I got to know the guys that were working underneath and the slinger. I started telling them jokes cos I was doing the clubs then.

Then I was asked to have a go on the cantilevers. I was a bit worried because you had climb the ladder and when you get on that rung you don't let go. I got put with Oxo, everybody knew him as Oxo, I never really knew his real name. It was the first time I had slewed a crane.After a time you become quite adept....I could slew ..rack out ...and lift all at the same time and then you were going between staging pulls.

Then I got my own crane....when I knew it was mine I got some gash paint....done it out , put shelves up and that.I had pictures of my babies on the wall too. I boxed in my controls and I enjoyed it . The atmosphere of the place was beautiful.A carpet..and I had my little transistor radio and my lovely electric fire. It was home from home.

Billy Suckley, he had a bloody visitors book in his crane, if a welder or millwright came to the crane they had to sign his stupid book...sometimes you'd pay a visit yourself, sign the book and he'd get out the tea and sandwiches.

The fire was everything, it was the old element type that was always burning out...I used to fix it by pulling the two ends together using a pencil....every so often it became all repairs and you had to take it to the sparks to get it fixed.They would say..'you won't get this back until tomorrow...and that would be a disaster....no tea, no fry ups and cold in the cab.

I used to go every day to the butchers in the old market in Hamilton Square and as soon as the guy saw me he would give me a quarter of Lockwoods beef. Not pork.The beef cost one and six. I'd have my dinner when I got back at one o'clock...frying pan on ,ladle on. Every driver, no matter whose crane you were on, would always leave tea, sugar,milk, bread and butter...a bit of bacon , eggs....they'd always have a fry up when they came on...that was cranedrivers policy.

The men below used to appreciate us having a radio too...if a big race was on ..say the Derby or something....you'd put the 1st ,2nd and 3rd out on your blackboard and you'd see their faces going " Oh Jesus!

They were like ants walking about below, and as time went by you went through the seasons.You saw the poor guys on the O.E.D. all muffled up working in ice and fog and freezing cold but you were OK 'cos you were in a warm cabin. You didn't need gloves and your feet were never cold. When the frost was really heavy you couldn't lower your block. It would freeze solid. You had to get a bit of cotton waste, set fire to it and lower it down on a wire. Some times you'd let your block go and then you'd see it break. Then you were happy.

When it was foggy you couldn't work at all...you were all wrapped up in the fog around you ..warm and snug. I used to get odd bits of hard wood from the Joiners shop and then I started to whittle between lifts and that. There was plenty of foreigners going on in the yard.. pokers for the fender and that sort of thing. There was a guy on nights ..a welder .. who used to do the wrought iron gates. They'd measure the width, guillotine the rods, put your house number on it and load them

23

into a van and away out of the yard.

We didn't have gas fires at home in them days so everyone would always take a bundle of cockwood home for the fire every night...any old bits of wood would do...old bits of slipway were the best as they were impregnated with tar and that. All hands would always walk out with a bundle of cockwood.

When you lived in Liverpool you jumped on the bus and all hands would go for the train at James Street Station, down in the lift and then onto the Rock Ferry train. Off at Green Lane Station and there was one big rush..there were so many men then....and then the same thing coming home. There were hundreds trying to get into those big old lifts with the folding doors at James Street ..and the little guy that was trying to take the tickets as everyone rushed past him always looked ever so disappointed. One day I heard a fella at the back shouting and complaining...'can't we get any more on ?

and the collector shouted..

'if you'd all get rid of your f.... cockwood we could. '

Pay day was the big queue, a little shed it was, you check your money and were happy that you hadn't had a day out. You had a few bob and you were happy. So you may go for a pint at the Castle. There were three pubs...the Castle...the Shakespeare and the King Alfred...mostly gone now when they built the new tunnel roads.

It was a dangerous place too...one guy was killed on nights...fell into the tank of a ship..I think it was a tanker...they reckoned he'd thought he'd seen a plank but it had been a shadow and he stepped. I had to pick up the stretcher cradle and lower it down...when he came up I could only see his head and I knew he was dead. He was hanging on the end of my block and I felt so sorry for him. When I went back on the next night the ship was all lit up like Blackpool.

You always had an old coat up the crane to use when you were greasing...and you had to tie yourself onto the crane rails whenever you went for a pee by using the old coat...it was very important to make sure which way the wind was blowing before you had a pee!

..I remember as a kid looking out over the river...you'd see New Brighton Tower and these bloody big things shaped like a letter Tee. I found out that they were cranes but I never thought

I would drive one of them.

I regret leaving a lot of good mates behind...they all knew their jobs..I reckon the worst thing they ever did was amalgamating with Vickers...Lairds could fly their own flag without any help from anybody.

I miss my crane, it was my last main job,...my working life had died...because I've no chance of going back to Lairds and standing there and saying...'I drove that crane' or ' I stood there and watched the launch of the so and so...

When you love a thing the money is secondary....it comes from the heart...you love your job and the power to do it....when somebody asks me where I worked I don't say " I used to work in Birkenhead "...I tell them the whole thing...." I used to drive a crane in Cammell Lairds. "

The Royal Castle Hotel, directly opposite what used to be the Cammell Laird main gate at the bottom of Green Lane.

Typical slipway cantilever cranes, shown here at the launch of RMS Windsor Castle in 1959.

John Cropper

Aged 51
Electrician
Served Apprenticeship in
Lairds 1957-1962
Worked in Lairds
1957-1971 and 1986 -1993

I was convinced that it wasn't the job for me...I wanted to be a butcher, but my father persuaded me to go down to Lairds. I didn't have the interview for the job, my Dad had to have it for me.

My Dad used to get me up for work every morning at ten to seven. I'd say...I'm coming down now Dad. Seven o'clock came and I was still getting up. Ten past seven and still getting up and then I'd bring my clothes down and get changed in front of the fire. I used to go to work with my Dad down Union Street in the morning and we were walking four deep, a yard behind four other people. Union Street and New Chester Road was full and we used to turn off down Seabank Road, down past the old leather works and then run to the clock.

I remember going down for the first time , it was so strange. I was introduced to the foreman after getting my papers from personnel. He took me round the workshop and then left me with an electrician, an ex RAF man who knew his job very well, I was with him for six months. I was making copper busbars for a submarine at the time...the O class subs I think they were. I was just picking up the job and then after six months it was my time to go out on the ships.

My first ship I remember was the Rockhampton Star. I was put with an electrician who I had heard gave his apprentices a hard time. I was dreading going outside because I didn't know what to expect. He was good at his job and quick, don't forget it was all piecework then, and you got more if you could get a good price from the ratefixer and then do the job as quickly as possible. You couldn't slack, if you slacked you lost money.

It wasn't like it is today where everything is cut for you and labelled and marked...then we had to measure our own cable runs on the boat, walk all the way to the Seabank Road end of the yard to the cable stores, taking your own jacks even, then get the cable right off the drum. If there was snow and ice on it, it was your job and you did it because you were on piecework. Then we had to get them shipped to the gangway and wait our turn for the crane to lift them aboard. Then uncoil, pull them into position,tie and clip them up to where you wanted.

I remember we had a boss called Mr.Cooper. He was a good man in so much that he was fair and he got the job done. You always knew when he'd left the shop and was heading for the boat, for some reason word always got through, I don't know if it was telepathy or not, but word got through he was on his way and it made people work just that little bit harder knowing that he was coming aboard. You wouldn't see him all the time, you might be working on the staging under the cable runs.. you'd just see him looking at you sometimes. He'd just look. No smile. Just a wink and off he'd go. He knew who the workers were and who the shirkers were did Mr.Cooper.

As a young lad we'd play daft games on the ship , like bull-dog fights. Bull-dog was what the laggers used on the cement over the asbestos sheets. I had a few good pals then

29

apprentices. I remember one day, it was the launch of the Windsor Castle. It was a beautiful day and about five or six of us went over the wall as we weren't too interested in the actual launch. Because it was such a good day we ended up at Harrison Drive beach and stayed there until after 7 o'clock at night. We had no plans to go there and even had to go to one of the lads houses' to get a pair of shorts because we didn't have any shorts with us. My mother, at home in Lower Tranmere, off Union Street, was frantic because she didn't know where I was. We eventually came home sunburnt but they're the kind of times we had.

That was a ship that really sticks out in my mind, the Windsor Castle. I worked on that from when I was 17 till it was fitted right through. I had a good 18 months on that ship and learnt an awful lot. She was a masterpiece of a job, the workmanship was superb, all over , from the engine room up. Every worker made the job what it was, fitters, joiners, there were master joiners then,and the french polishers too. Everywhere was immaculate. To see that job at the end of the day you had to be proud of it.

Christmastime was good too, usually a big piss-up. We used to go to the Chester Arms in the Haymarket, facing the old market before they built the tunnel approach roads. We'd go there , spend a lot of time there, and then walk around the market intoxicated then up Grange Road, then generally drift in the direction of home. It was a very close knit place then , almost like a family.

Later on I was lucky enough to go on sea trials with the bulk carriers Irish Star and Star Arcadia, roughly 17 days to Norway. I was the only engine room spark and the foreman spark, Roy Vernon, was taking care of the deck. I'd just finished my dinner and was sitting on a switchboard mat. I was just sitting there because I wasn't a very good sailor, when this chargehand fitter, Frankie Rowan , came up to me with a bottle of beer in his hand and he was going from side to side. I took one look at him and had to go back up top to be sick.I was lying on my bunk when everywhere went quiet. Ray Vernon came in and said that the ship was in darkness, just bobbing around, no power no nothing. He said we'd have to get the gennies back on the board as they weren't coming in. I said ..'but Ray I'm sick'. Sick or not though we had to do something so we went down and put the gennies back on the board, got the lights on, got the diesel going first then the alternators and got the ship back in order. Everyone cheered and that was a nice feeling ..then I was sick again !

We had our sad times too in Lairds. I remember as a lad we had a foreman spark called Billy Daley . Billy would always say good morning to everyone, apprentices too. He'd said good morning to me one day and by nine o'clock that morning he was dead. 42 years old. His wife used to work in the offices at Lairds and she gave his tools out to all the apprentices. She gave me a set square and I've still got it to this day.

I took my wife to the last launch, the submarine Unicorn, the first one she's ever seen. My family and friends got some idea of life in Lairds. But my time is coming soon I know. There's hardly anyone there anymore. Once you couldn't walk ten yards without getting stopped to talk. Now you just walk around the yard...today I counted 12 people walking in the yard as far as the eye could see.

I thought I'd finish my days off there. That's how I felt...I could give another 20 years to shipbuilding and look what's happened. I blame VSEL and the government. They have known about our problems for years now and could have helped Lairds survive.

I don't like the prospect of not working, because I've always worked, my whole life. When the time comes to get the tap on the shoulder, even though you know it's coming, I feel that if I'd only been there a week it's as if it was a lifetime and it will still hurt me. I'll still feel that gut feeling when I get the phone call to go and see the boss who'll say ' your times up John', I'll still feel sad. I'll accept it but I'll be hurting inside.

I'll never forget Lairds. It may be a long time dead but never forgotten. Nobody will ever forget Lairds, especially people in Birkenhead. It'll never come back but it will always stick in my mind.

The RMS Windsor Castle, often described as the last great passenger liner of it's era.

The Manor Arms in Union Street Birkenhead. Once a busy throughfare to the shipyard.

Joe Bennett
Aged 79
Sailor Gang

Worked in Lairds
1947-1978

I started as a platers helper on 11s 4d per week. That was pretty good when you compared it to 8s or 9s running errands in a shop or somewhere like that. I had to go round with a journeyman carrying all the gear, all the tools and that and we went from job to job.

Later on I was at sea as a deck boy but eventually came back to Lairds when I was out of work...you just went down on the stand at Lairds. That was by the old St. Marys graveyard in Abbey Street...they all used to stand about six deep...you might get picked, you might not... you might get a few days or a week. It was just all men standing there waiting, the boss would come out....you, you and you...and that was it. A boss called Harold Allison used to look after the labourers side and if he knew you'd been away to sea he'd say come on we want you.

After the war I went on the ferries, then a pal of mine said to get into Lairds..docking ships with carpenters...we got the same money as them. After a while that was knocked in the head when the carpenters kicked up hell.

I used to go out for a night docking on my bike, later

on they had a little mini runabout that would pick you up...Billy Cook used to drive it, he was very conscientious was Billy..so much so that he'd often knock on the wrong bloody door at 2.00 in the morning , some not very happy people around then. So I always made him pick me up on the end of our road. I'd go down about 10 to 1 and many a time the police would stop and ask what you were up to. A mate of mine was pulled on his way home about 3.30 in the morning in Beckwith Street....Where have you been ? they asked him.....he said he'd been docking a ship at Cammell Lairds. They took him back to Lairds and checked with the gateman who backed up his story. 'That's OK then' says the coppers...'make your own way home' and they just left him there.

There were quite a lot of ex-seamen in the shipwrights labourers and the sailor gang. One of the sailor gangs main jobs would be to take out and then reposition the dry dock caissons when a ship came in or out of dry dock. Most of these were at night say 3.00 am...you'd go out from home at about 11.00pm and then you'd be on the old turntable on top of the caisson...allowing the water to run in from the river...as we waited for it to fill up to about 12 foot we'd be just standing by and would go down and fall asleep on the ropes...then they'd blow all the water out and the caisson would slowly come up like a ship. We'd wait until the grooves at the sides were free and then using ropes and block and tackle would take it round and nestle it on the wall just alongside the dock.

When the ship was in it was all done in reverse...but that was trickier...there could be wedges and all sorts floating around and if they got stuck in the sealing grooves at either side of the caisson then it was a problem. It was a very tight fit ...it had to be to keep the river water out...you had to slowly worm it into position.

One time at night we had two brothers working with

us, Arthur and Lennie Smith. Somebody threw a heaving line to Lenny and the next thing was he shot right down this groove into the dock, right down, and his brother was panicking, we were worried about him getting crushed by the caisson. We shouted to the lads on the other side to hold everything and that was struggle, there's a lot of deadweight in those caissons. We managed to throw him a rope in the dark and pull him out. He was pretty shocked as you can imagine.

On the odd occasion we were a sort of skeleton crew...there were a couple of submarines for the Israelis in for repair once and they had no crew, so four of us would man them to take them into dry dock. We were lent out sometimes for a launch, especially if it was big one like the Mauritania or the Ark Royal or the Windsor Castle. Then they'd want about 40 men on deck, tying up and fendering them in as they came round the knuckle of the wet basin.

The best job as far as I was concerned was unrigging ships and putting it back up again. We used to take it to a place in the New Yard, all the blocks off the derricks and that....when they came back we would grease them all up, put new split pins in them and hang them up, the crane would pull them up for us.

I got married in 1944 and we managed to scrape along. I tried Vauxhalls once when Vauxhalls first came and I got taken on, but when I looked at the money and what I was getting in Lairds and said to myself forget it. I think there was about 3d or 4d difference. And then I had to go on shift work and I didn't know how the hell I was going to get there because I didn't have a car, just an old Lambretta scooter. So I stayed at Lairds, I knew what I was doing, I was near as I lived in Priory Street. I really liked working in the yard. There was plenty of activity and all that. You knew everybody, the same crowd of fellas all the while.

We organised days out to the races and that. We had a sort of sweep thing, the sailor gang and the Joiners labourers. If one person won that was it but if more than one won then it went into a kitty, then we had a three man committee who organised it at the end of the year. Once we went to Llandudno and Aber falls...we'd organise a coach and a meal then they'd drop us off at a pub on the way home and we'd have a bit of a booze up. Another time we went to Doncaster Races and we stopped at a place by Skipton, then on to the races then a pub at night.

I've been finished a long time now and I'm glad I'm not trying to make my way in the world at this moment because I feel sorry for the kids leaving school. I feel sorry for the poor kids now. I'm glad I'm not at work now the way things are. I can't see Lairds building any more ships now. Lairds did a wonderful job for this town and it's bad to see them going the way they have. I remember them building the 1000th ship, and during the war they were turning out one a month.

In the war I was going in convoys out of this river. If they ever do have another war, and I hope they don't .... they'll miss Lairds.

HMS Audacious coming into dry dock circa 1913. A floating dock gate or Caisson can be seen in the background.

Launch of HMS Ark Royal, May 3rd 1950. Launched by HM the Queen

Arnie Locker

Aged 61
Engineer

Worked in Lairds
1957-1980
1988-1993

I was 25 when I went to Lairds. My father was a coppersmith there for most of his life, his greatest claim to fame was that he did the voice pipes on the Mauritania. He brought up nine kids on Cammell Lairds wages. He worked an awful lot of overtime. He tried to get out of Lairds in 1940 to join the R.A.F. but they found out about it and you weren't allowed to leave Lairds in wartime. My uncle Billy too brought up three girls on Lairds, he worked there until the day he died.

I was quite taken aback when I first went to Lairds because there were 12 to 13,000 people there then, and the rush into and out of the yard had to be seen to be believed. We lived in Liverpool then and I came in on the train. It was 7d a day return and you had to be in before 7.30 am.

I started in the drawing office as a draughtsman, we used to work on big 10 foot drawing boards and worked on a drawing for up to three months because you had to detail everything. When I first went in I was put on the standard squad as an improver as I hadn't been used to technical drawing, I'd been away at sea. I started on £11-18s per week. You had to learn the basics. Every ship that Lairds had built in the past the blueprints were down in the safe. Lairds made and built everything on a ship in those days. If a ship was at sea and something went down,say just a valve or something, the shipowners would get in touch with Lairds and ask for a replacement. Then we'd go down and get the blueprints, draw up the valve on a fitting sheet, give it a number and out it would go to the shops. First the pattern shop to make a wooden pattern of it and then into the machine shop.It was a sort of after-sales service if you like.

The boss of the drawing office was a man called Wrightson, we all called him Buller 'cos he was always bullshitting. It was all very staid then. You virtually weren't allowed to take you jacket off. Certainly no smoking, and if you were talking to someone in the office Buller would slide up to you from nowhere and he just whispered in your ear...' I hope you're talking about the job'...just like that. I always remember one lad who came in to the office with a red shirt on one day and he was sent home to change it. We were all expected to wear a collar and tie, white shirt, soberly dressed.

You had to go in once a year to see Buller and beg for a merit rise. It was always 26 pound a year. If you were exceptionally good you might get 50 pound a year but that was very rare. I always remember a guy had been in to see Buller and asked him for a rise because he'd been there a while and never had a rise. This guy came out and said that Buller had told him he was a good lad and was doing alright and he was going to get a rise. I was in with Buller after that and he said to me....' Who was that who just went out ?'....He'd given him a load of bull and he didn't even know who he was talking to.

The conditions in the drawing office weren't that good, poor lighting and the heating wasn't much good either, but out on the ships, especially on the slipways, things were pretty grim, considering that the men had big unions things were bloody awful. I always remember old Charlie Chase, he was a big blocker man,, he'd go round kicking all their billy cans over if they hadn't got their tea made within the 10 minutes. There was nowhere to hand your clothes, and they walked out of that shipyard with shitty greasy clothes on, covered in grease or red lead and that was then put on all the ferries, the seats on the trains and the trams, because you went home the way you were dressed. They could come off the gangway on a Friday afternoon and get a D.C.M , just like that!

I've still got an old Lairds Rule book...it gives a list of offences that you could be done for....dismissal or a fine....... waiting around furnaces...Christ they were bloody freezing and just keeping warm...... Loafing in a compartment of a ship other than the one you were working in....playing cards....fighting....sleeping.... preparing for meals.... leaving ships other than by gangways......SNOWBALLING !, stone throwing and believe it or not, bathing in the dock!

Of course you need some rules because shipbuilding is one of the most dangerous occupations you can imagine. On a tanker the holds could be 100 feet deep and you're on staging that could be a bit 'iffy', so your life was on the staging. Even today on a submarine you're dancing around the staging, balancing on and off. There's people working above you and people working below you and people working in confined spaces and noise all around you. The closest call I ever had was on the British Lion. We'd had a successful sea trials . Nothing had gone wrong and we were waiting at the Mersey bar to de-ballast before coming up the river. Me and a fella called Roger Smith had been getting the gear off the propeller shaft that we used to monitor the shaft speed and the slip across the gearbox, it was all part of the sea trial records. The main engines that we were standing alongside began to run away, the noise was terrible...all the crankcase doors were flying past us in slow motion, all over the engine room. The pedestal bearing and the main shaft into the gearbox was just ripped aside and thrown onto the gratings were we had been working. There was no fire but oil everywhere and fortunately it didn't ignite. That was the nearest I ever came to a disaster.

After trials and other times we'd have a few beers. We used to have some great times, meeting up in all the pubs, The Old House at Home, The Harp and all them, some fells never got further than the Castle, especially at Christmas. One time I never got further than the Castle. Everyone always ended up going home rotten drunk or staggering round Birkenhead looking for the wife's Christmas present. You'd be in and out of Woolies a dozen times wondering what to buy, or buying the same present twice.

The worst of it is that those pubs are still full up today and have been for the last three or four months, as they have their redundancy parties they take over the pub. I don't know how it's going to affect me when I finally finish up because I'm brainwashed into getting up every morning at 6.15 am and going out to work and coming back home. I've lived ships all my life. I don't really know anything else but ships . There's a lot of good characters in shipbuilding and there's some funny fellas too. They're all good lads , everyone to a man.

The Britannia, halfway down Green Lane towards Lairds main gate. Now closed.

The Harp. Chamberlain Street / Old Chester Road.

The Old House at Home Chamberlain Street.

Gerry O'Neill

Aged 65
Plumber

Worked in Lairds
1940-1984

I started two days before my 14th birthday in July. The weather was beautiful. It was a job. As simple as that. My Dad used to clean the windows for somebody that was in the piecework office in the yard and he asked him if he could fix me up.

I started in the time office as an office boy, you had to be in before the men, at 7.00 a.m.. If a timekeeper happened to sleep in, Walter Robinson , the boss, would say to you "slip up to the Joiners shop son, so and so hasn't turned in, and you had to do that time clock..in those days if you weren't there for seven o'clock you weren't there, you'd be docked half a day.

I really wanted to be a Joiner, purely because I was put on the Joiners clock for my last 12 months as an office boy and all my mates were Joiners. I went to see the boss Joiner ..Davies..I can see him now ..white haired in a blue suit, stiff collar and black tie. I asked him what were the chances of becoming a Joiner. Nothing doing at all son he says. So I thought, that's a bit of a kick in the teeth, and I hadn't got a clue from there on. What do I do now ..be a bus conductor or a railway driver? The lad that had left the time office just before me had gone to the plumbers. I thought well, he's brighter than me so there must be something in this plumbing lark.

I went to see old Tommy Collerton, and rhetoric was never really Toms thing, he was an expert at nodding. I said good morning Mr. Collerton any chance of starting as an apprentice plumber Sir?

It was always Sir in those days. So he says...when are you 16 son?

Next week Sir.

Right O , come and see me next week and I'll fix you up.

Now as a kid of 16 you're not thinking now is this good or bad, so I promptly go home to my mum and tell her that I'm starting as an apprentice plumber on the 20 something of January.

My mum asks me If I have it in writing.

No ..I just have to go on Monday.

Now on the strength of this she has to go out and get me a couple of pairs of boots and a pair of overalls, 'cos I haven't got any of this tackle and you don't realise at the time that nobody has got that sort of money to be buying brand new boots and that. I confess that when it got to Monday morning I thought what if he doesn't give me a job ?

So I arrived on Monday morning and knocked on his door very politely went in and said......'You said you'd give me a start this morning as an apprentice plumber Sir'

"That's right son"...he'd got the note made out already. "Slip across to the time office and they'll fix you up."

My first few days were with a decent enough fella'....my first job was the overflow drains from the turbine plant down the bottom of the Brass Shop. Well, my overalls didn't get too badly damaged did they.

After that we they were building a new toilet on the corner of where the old ambulance room was...but first they were building a new managers toilet...it was like a bungalow.. Now to get the water for it they had to get the water from what was the old ship electricians shop. We had to dig a trench and I ended up to my waist in solid bloody clay...it was piddling down and we're in the ground putting two inch steel pipe in the ground. I go home that night in a right mess and my mum says....'You can pack that bloody job up.'

It was quite frightening really..as a young lad I was petrified in some ways.....I was fortunate in being in the offices first...they had proper toilets..at least they had a door on it...but in the plumbers shop they had a long trough along one side of the room and another on the other side for piddling in. My mother had always said to never expose yourself in front of another man.

So the first time I had to go I saw all these men sitting in a row like a load of budgies discussing Tranmere Rovers, Liverpool, and asking each other for lights. Well the first time you drop your pants in front of a crowd you know it's a terrible, terrible experience. When I tell people now they think its disgraceful but nobody took a blind bit of notice.

Another time when I was a lad I was with a plumber, on the new Seabank Road toilets, 6 inch flush pipes they were and about 8 foot long...the plumber says...right son , you get one and I'll get one...all the way from the North Yard to Seabank Road. I had a bloody sore shoulder that day.Those toilets were a bit upmarket then..white porcelain troughs and partitions between the cubicles so you had your bit of space, but still no doors.

During the war,Lairds wouldn't let you use the war as an excuse you know, it wouldn't interfere with work. I remember the only thing you would really notice is that sometime somebody would be missing and the poor bugger had probably been killed or his family had been killed and they go missing, permanent. I don't think anyone wanted to think about it too much in case it happened to them. There was a girl, a lovely girl, that I knew. She worked in the stationery department . She lost her family in Well Lane, Rock Ferry. A land mine dropped on a row of houses and she was the only survivor. But Lairds as a yard didn't suffer that much during the blitz.

Although they (the enemy) did succeed with the Prince of Wales when she was in the basin. A bomb had gone between it and the basin wall and blew a sea valve or something and she flooded and was literally leaning on the engine shop wall at one stage. We used the battleship as an air raid shelter so you're fairly happy with 14 inches of steel above you.

I'm sure that we built a few boats twice in rapid succession because they went out and went missing.They were waiting out at the Mersey bar and sometimes a ship would leave the yard and then goodnight.

Because of the blackout you started later when it was daylight. The yard couldn't be thoroughly blacked out you see., and when it went dark early in the winter they weren't allowed to have lights...so it would make for shorter days but it extended the working week to 6 or 7 days...even as an office lad I worked from 7-9 at night four nights a week.

Later on I was made chargehand. I had seen lads younger than me, I was 24, being made up, and was beginning to see my bum a bit. I was on the bench lead burning and doing old fashioned plumbing as well as they were building the Isle of Man boats then...although people speak about plumbers never doing any real plumbing work I used more hundredweights of solder in that month than many a plumber had seen in their careers. So I'm thinking, every bastards getting jobs except me.

Then one morning the boss came up and said that the

head man wants you to go and teach at the night school. So I went up to Birkenhead Tech. and did a full season on 1st, 2nd and 3rd year practical plumbing. At the time I was one of the oddballs that had been to night school, and I had to go on Sunday afternoons because of the blackout. I stuck this for a little while but could see it was shaping up as a full time job which wasn't for me. I was getting the homework in on the back of Woodbine packets you know, or they just wouldn't turn up.

Tommy Collerton sent for me one day and said.....you can pack that job up 'cos you're starting as chargehand on Monday. It was an amazing thing, 'cos nobody trains you anything, training is the in thing now but then all of a sudden from being one of 90 fellas who were saying what a stupid bastard the boss was, Monday morning you're the stupid bastard. In six months I got made up to foreman. I inherited a chargehand who was the original awkward arse, eventually he had to be nailed down, but I managed to nurse the other class 1 plumber/welders around to my side. I just had to keep one foot firmly in place on the back of their neck.

Looking back today its surprising how little feeling I have for it now. How many times has it wanted saving ? Three to my knowledge. Quite frankly I think Lairds lost its way. I believe it may have shut around 1960 or whatever the precise date was..when they ran out of work. We had one boat we were building for the Canadian Navy and that was our last order...finito...and then there was some hope that we might get involved with the Polaris contract and we did. We got the crumbs from Vickers table..

If I had to write an epitaph for Cammell Lairds it would be that in the end I think that Lairds got what it deserved.

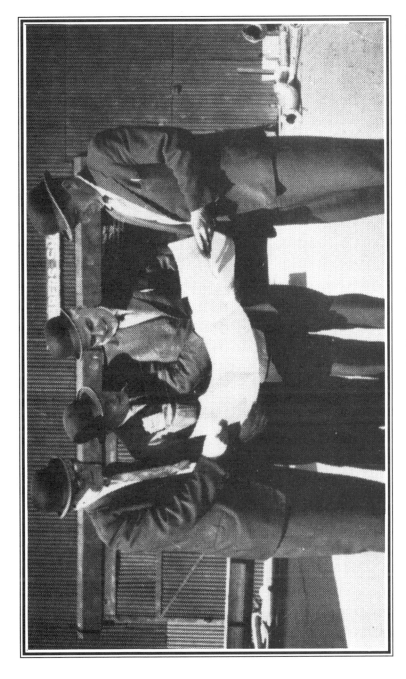

Some 'Blocker Men', outside the old Plumbers Shop, looking at a plan for the camera. Gerry O'Neill is on the far right.

John Swift

Aged 62

Caterer

Worked in Lairds
1971-1993

My first memories of Lairds was when I was a child. I was born in New Ferry and our garden used to go down to the river. We used to walk along the wall looking towards Cammell Lairds. I used to look out of my bedroom window and see the boats that were out there, on the river and in Lairds .Your imagination runs amok as a child and I just wanted to be there. When other kids were kicking a ball around I was making little boats. So really when I came to work there it was in a funny way a bit like coming home.

Later on when I was seagoing, I remember waiting for the bus at Woodside to go home when the shiprepair yard were letting out. I just saw a mass of what I used to think were dirty, greasy, oily people. When I was offered this job in 1971 I came to have a look around and was pleasantly surprised in as much as they had built modern canteens. It was the same warm feeling again then. A felling of, very quickly, a sense of belonging which I hadn't had before in previous jobs.

At 9.00am on my first day I was taken by the Personnel Manager to the kitchens and I met the supervisors. I remember one of the canteen assistants came across to me and said..

'Would you like a cup of tea luv and I hope your going to be happy here'. I thought....well, what a change. She knew I was going to be the new boss but there was this warmth which having been away from Merseyside you tend to forget.

Not long after a ship was going on its sea trials and the ships Manager, Tommy Naylor, asked me to come and see him. I didn't know what to expect. He said to me.....'You're new here and I thought you should have someone you can contact and who will help you and I'm your man, I'll give you all the help I can.' That was the sort of feeling you got from everyone there.If anyone could help you they would.

Ships trials was a busy time for everyone, but from my point of view it was like squeezing a quart into a pint pot. A merchant ship that might have a seagoing crew of between 35 and 45 men might have as many as 180 men as a trials crew, so we'd need temporary accommodation, taking over laundry rooms and recreation spaces. Obviously the Galley would be going at full blast and of course you'd get breakdowns and that was what it was all about, just as much as if it was part of the engine.

I had to try to gauge what a trial would need to cater for everyone aboard and I remember one time the trial was almost over and we were off the Mersey Bar. The stores were looking about right and the only thing we had a lot of was bread. Bread and milk was always a difficult thing to judge. We had about 40 loaves that we didn't need so we decided to feed the seagulls. It had been a beautiful, really glorious day when Lo! and behold thick fog came down and we couldn't get in. So you can imagine how I felt about feeding the seagulls. That was certainly a lesson. Never let go of anything until you get in.

We had females on our trials too, I think we were the only company in the country to do that. One woman, Lois, used to sing and dance for all hands. They kept up morale on hard heavy trials, even the language was moderated a bit. The men are more cheerful and I found it worked very well. Once,on one of the Frigates, maybe it was the Liverpool, they'd have the swimmer of the watch. He's the man who goes in if somebody goes overboard. He takes a line and recovers the man overboard. One of the waitresses was on the bridge getting ready to serve the Captain with his morning coffee and they decided they were going to do this man overboard exercise.

The Frigate was stopped and the man overboard turned out to be the youngest sailor on the ship, only 17. He was recovered by the on watch swimmer and they came up on the bridge. In the meantime someone shouted why doesn't the Skipper go in ? So with no more ado the Skipper went in. He too ended up back on the bridge and they were all dripping wet. The Lairds waitress goes to give them a cup of coffee and the Captain goes to take it. She said, to the Captain of a Royal Navy vessel,......'This isn't for you, it's for that poor young lad there....fancy sending him out there like that!' And he saw the funny side of it too.

Back in the yard in the early days some parts of the catering left a lot to be desired. One of the bones of contention, quite rightly too, was that we had different classes of feeding in there.

We'd feed about 1,000 in the works canteen, 400 to 500 in the staff, and then managers. There was the Junior mess which had two sittings of about 80 each, and the senior mess which was about 60 and then there was what we called the Golden Trough which was for the Directors. In the Senior, No.1 mess, there was waitress service , they didn't pay for their food and had a free can of beer. In the No.2 mess they paid for their food. If a man got into the No.1 mess then they were really on the up and up. The Golden Trough for the

Directors had a beautiful walnut table, a cocktail bar and silver service. I think there were about 12 in all.

We've all got the same stomachs and we should have a democratic feeding system.Graham Day realised this in 1972 and changed things. The only thing you have to make allowances for was to have a non-overall area. I think that the trade unions recognised this and that we were really trying to give everyone value for money. It took a few months of settling in but in the end we worked it out..I think that the men could see that we were trying to make everyone equal.

The really big occasions were the launch functions, we've had some VIPs there, the Prince and Princess of Wales once. It wasn't like a hotel where everything is stitched up with Headwaiters and his waiters and a master of ceremonies. I had three really skilled people with me who could hold their own with cooks, if not chefs, and the others too first class canteen workers. We had to be jacks of all trades with a lot of preparation and a lot of thinking about what you do.I often had a couple of sleepless nights beforehand but it had to be right.

This meant that I missed most of the launches but we'd always do all the bunting for the bottle, decorate it and that. I did see some and there was always a deep sense of pride when you see the ship starting on the slipway or in the hall as it is now. You'd seen it building up and building up and you'd identify with it. Feel a sense of , although I've not been on it, it certainly belongs to me.

Now it's very sad when I've had to tell people that they're going, who've worked for me for years and I choke.I know that I'll be going myself too. We've had two years to condition ourselves for this terrible time at the end. You think you're conditioned to it but we kid ourselves.

Britains first Guided Missile Destroyer, HMS Devonshire. Here just after her launch in 1960.

HMS Liverpool minutes before her launch.

John Haggerty

Aged 70
Boilermaker-Welder

Worked in Lairds
1939-1959
1962-1964
1965-1980

My family came from Jarrow which was a shipbuilding town. A big firm at the time was Jarrow Partners...they were on their last legs then during the hard times in 1937/1938.

I worked as a lad of 14 in Black Dyke Mills...there was no work on Tyneside. It was noisy, like the shipyard but very different.The department I was in was where they washed the wool before they sent it out.Before we knocked off we used to go in there and plunge our hands into the huge vats. You didn't need a wash. 'Course I had hands like a girl in those days.

We came down to Birkenhead to get my Dad work..he was a riveter, a holder-up. I didn't even know what a welder was, but my Dad said to go as a welder. I knew about the noise 'cos I had been down here as a schoolboy in the holidays and had brought my Dads butties down to him. He was working on a whaler and god did it stink. He was explaining his job to me. He switched his hammer on a few times and the noise was deafening. In those days you could be in a tank with 3 or 4 riveting squads and 3 or 4 caulkers. Of course that's why most boilermakers are deaf now.

I remember my Dad telling me ' Never forget son that when you are in Lairds you'll only be a number son, no matter what your job is, and you can be sacked on the spot.

When I first went to Lairds I wouldn't take my gloves off , even to eat my butties. I was terrified of getting my hands dirty.I remember my dad taking me down there on my first day, he left me outside the main shop and said that the boss welder would come down. I remember standing there outside the office looking at all the sparks flying around from the burners and the welders and all the row going on. This little fat man came up to me..

'You John Haggerty ?

' Yes'

'Well I'm Mr. Simpson...the boss.....put that fag out !'

I was taken over to the welding bay and introduced me to a chargehand who put me with a welder as a can lad. I was 16 then. About ten to nine the welder told me to go and make a brew. I didn't know what he meant. He told me that it was to make tea. I said ' I didn't come here to make tea, I came to be a welder.' Little did I know that was part of the job. And a very important part too.

What did shock me the first time was the toilets.It was just a long open trough.They did have cubicles but there were no doors on them. You had to give your number into the bloke there who put it down in his book. You were only allowed 4 or 6 minutes in there, I can't exactly remember now. If you were any longer the bloke would play hell with you.

After a while in the bays they sent me out onto a merchant ship and then onto the Prince of Wales, she was like a floating palace compared to a merchant ship. I used to get lost frequently. One particular job I had on the B barbette, from the gun turret to the base of the ship..with all the different lifts that fetch the shells up too. Well , I was on that for months and months but when I first went on it, for the first couple of weeks I used to get lost. I'd come up for a brew , take the wrong turn and end up in A barbette.

She was bomb damaged at some time. I think it exploded between the shipside and the basin wall. She was keeled over on the quay wall...we weren't allowed on her for a while then.

When we were on nights everything was blacked in.You had to make sure no lights were left on when you went off the main deck down below. We had to do firewatch one night a month. That was the worst time really, pretty dangerous. Say you were working outside and something went wrong with your cable or supply line,then you had try and trace the cable in the dark. There could be anything up to 100 cables on the go and they all came out at more or less the same place. So you were going down, trying to find your way down a ladder or the staging and still keep hold of your cable, working you way back to your box.It could be risky, especially around Christmas, 'cos you'd always get some who'd had a few.

Thinking back now the hours were unbelievable,on the Prince of Wales we worked, as apprentices, all day Monday,Tuesday...all night Wednesday, all day Thursday, all Friday night..Saturday Morning..and all Sunday. On Saturday night we used to go off to the Tower in New Brighton for a dance and then turn in for work on Sunday.

I liked the launches at first, then you'd get a bit blase about then, especially during the war, they'd be throwing them out about three a week. Later on I used to take my son John down to launches...I wouldn't say anything about it but he'd hear about it in school and ask me to take him down.

I was only a bad lad once and was sacked for it. I slid out one day to the bank. Some foreman had seen me and that was that. Harry Johnson was the head boss..he says to me

"Off the job this morning son. Sorry, I have to sack you.

Come back in a fortnight."

I came back , was started again, and my cable was still on the same job that I was on before.

I always seemed to go back to Lairds...I had a few sessions out but came back. One time I was looking to come back I was going past the back entry at Hamilton Square Station where my Dads boilermakers office was then, he became the District Delegate for the Boilermakers. There was a knock on the window and it was my Dad. I asked if there were any jobs going. He said there was not a job in the port. So the next morning I tried Lairds anyway. The boss told me to go back home and there would be a telegram there for me in the afternoon. There was and I started the next morning. I was happy, I enjoyed the work...it was a job I knew . I was good at my job and I got along with the people

It's hard to say why I liked it so much, especially as it wasn't that well organised. They'd have you working inside in the summer and outside in the winter...you'd be working outside round the after end on a butt...course all the staging planks would be covered in snow and you'd have to turn them over and they'd be sopping wet. You'd be sitting or kneeling on the plank all day long and your knees would be soaked. Water would be dripping from the planks above you and you could easily slip. Crazy I know ..but I liked it.

There was no way you could have a wash then or leave your gear anywhere so you came home in your dirty overalls looking a scruff. I always remember when I was living in Prenton Dell Road and I came home early one day. I was on the bus and just passing where Sainsburys is now. I saw my wife Peg and the two kids, Maureen and John. They were with another woman.

I jumped off the bus and gave her a kiss and said I'd go shopping with her.The woman she was with said " Are you going to let him come shopping with you looking like that ?"

Peg said "It's him looking like that means I can come out shopping !"

I only ever left Lairds for economic reasons..I never really wanted to leave Lairds...I learnt my trade from some of the best craftsmen in the world and became a craftsman myself,...though theoretically I couldn't tell you a thing about welding. But I knew I could go anywhere in the yard and do any job they asked me to.

We built the ships in Lairds despite the management not because of them. It was a good yard ruined by bosses.

I'll be sad, like most of my generation , when it goes. It will be catastrophic for the whole town.

I enjoyed all the time I was there.

HMS Prince of Wales at sea. The Barbettes that John Haggerty speaks of are directly underneath the gun turrets.

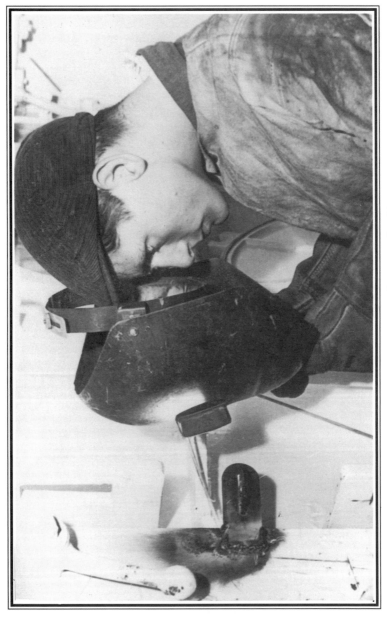

Welding in the confined spaces of a ship.

Joe Edwards

Aged 79
Electrician

Worked in Lairds
1936-1978

I'd served my time in shipping with Blue Funnel but really hadn't worked in a shipyard on new ships being built from scratch. Back in the 1930s conditions were very bad compared with later years. When you finished work you didn't have paper towels or anything like that to clean yourself up with. You had to travel back home with your overalls on. There was nowhere to lock you tools up or anything, you just had to take a chance on them being safe because they used to get broken into.

It was a different class of work then though, not the same as it is now. I was on the Ark Royal for twelve months and it was all lead covered cable then, the smaller cable anyway, and you could make a nice job of it. I used to drag the cable through a dry paraffin rag to straighten it and at the same time I'd polish it. By the time you got up the bulkhead and clipped it up with brass clips it looked a picture. It made your hands really black. Now of course we know that perhaps we shouldn't have been handling the lead like that, but I came up against worse things than that later on in Lairds, that's what it was like then.

There were some terrible cock-ups on the Ark Royal. When it was being built labour was in short supply then and Lairds were bringing people in from outside the area, Wigan and places like that. I don't think they'd ever seen a ship before. They'd give these fellas a job to do and tell them how to do it. Then when the time came to test it the bloody lot blew up and it all had to be done again. Bloody comedians they were

I liked working on Merchant work too, fitting out saloons and cabins. You'd see the ship being built up and up and then see the finished article. All the furniture goes in, curtains , the lot. On Admiralty work it was all iron and grey paint, with not a lot of comfort on the ship.

There wasn't a lot of comfort for anyone in the yard in those days, there was no official tea break morning or afternoon and there was a ships manager called Charlie Chase, that's what everyone called him but his real name was Wilson, he went to great pains to try to make sure you didn't get one either.

What the blokes used to do was use the old dried milk cans that used to be used for baby food. They'd get one of them and punch two holes in either side of it, then use a welding rod for the handle. They'd go to the burner and boil water up in these cans to make their tea. This Charlie Chase used to go all around the ship in every nook and cranny and if he saw anyone with these little kettles of tea he'd kick the cans over.

The worst time I had was when I lost the top off my thumb. I was in the workshop stripping down a very big motor, it was off a tanker. The labourer and I were trying to get the end plate of the bottom bearing which was about 15" diameter. We were striking the end plate on alternate sides with a shortened staging board to bump it off while the crane was holding the weight of the job on a chain. While we were bashing it the chain slipped and the whole job moved and rolled and chopped the end of my thumb off. I had to go to the hospital to get stitched up and was off for about a month. I didn't get paid for that time off. Eventually the union managed to get me compensation....£302.

A couple of weeks after my accident the whole ruling changed over accidents at work. It didn't really matter what happened then, the firm would be responsible. One bloke had an accident on the rag buff later on. Silly bugger tried to polish paper thin metal and it wrapped up on him as soon as the buff bit it. He gashed his hand and got £1000.

Looking back though I loved going to work. I'd get there half an hour early, before time. It wasn't a drudge to me. I'd go there sometimes when I wasn't really fit to go. I'd never backheel a job.

When I was in the workshops I used to do lots of little foreigners too. Hoovers, irons, hairdryers and that. I even had an artificial leg on my bench once, I riveted it up. Glasses came in to be fixed, wives charm bracelets the lot, I'd have a go at anything. Sometimes I'd make a bit of brassware too, jugs and poker stands, that sort of thing.

Foreigners apart though I always looked at any job as a job worth doing well. The way I looked at it, if a shipping owner was good enough to send work to our yard for building or repair to employ us then he deserved a bloody good job, so you do the job to the best of your ability.

When I retired I had 20 odd years in. When I was paid off in 1978 I was disappointed with the £2000 I got from Lairds. That included my holiday money and a week in hands money too. I was sad and disappointed.

I'm sad about things today too, the place has been going since old John Laird. It's been the mainstay of the town.

HMS Ark Royal in service.

Jack Rogers

Aged 61
Joiner

Worked in Lairds
1947-1953
1966-1993

I actually hated woodwork at school and still don't know why I became a Joiner. My Dad was a boss painter in Lairds and I just knew that I didn't want to be like him. The first day was a bit nervy. It was all so strange. In those days we had a big wooden triplane, a wooden jack plane and a wooden smoother. The first thing you had to do was sharpen them all up and then you had to take the wooden planes over to the paint shop where there was a big vat of linseed oil and leave them in that for a week. They were then brought back and put on your bench until they dried out. You didn't do a lot on your first day just sharpen your gear up.

The first job they used to give you was sandpapering. In those days the ship was a mass of wood. All the beads and polish work was always given to the first year lad, then after about 12 months you were expected to do the same work as the journeyman who'd perhaps been at it for 30 years.

I was put with a great big fella who was Jewish, Jack Rimmer was his name, he had a whacking big nose and he chewed tobacco. He used all my brand new tools that I was issued with, they were free like, yours when you signed your indentures and finished your time. I think I've got a small square of oilstone left, the rest wasn't really up to much. Then I was shifted around a bit in the shop. They started you off on small jobs and gradually went to putting furniture together, wardrobes, chests of drawers and desks.

The joiners shop was a little world on its own, the manager, Sammy Davies was really strict and the shop foreman and chargehand made our lives murderous then. I've been a chargehand myself since then and but never had the power that these fellas had in the 1940s. He could come up to you and if you back chatted them they could send you home for a week. You got no money and the shop stewards never intervened. Eventually I went out onto the ships and that was a totally different environment from the shop.

On the ships the foreman called you by your first name, it was like growing up a bit you know, they'd show a lot more interest in you and go into detail explaining what's required of you on the ship, where you start and that. The attitude of the men outside was totally different.

It was one of the apprentices jobs to make the tea but tea was a definite no go, the apprentice had to run the gauntlet of the blocker men.In them days if you saw a blocker he was a boss, no matter who he was, and he was looking for you. So we had different ways of making tea, either put it on the hot fire and keep your eyes peeled or go to the platers shed and put the can in front of the furnace doors.

One day I'm standing by the furnace with half a dozen other lads and a shout goes up....'Here's Charlie Chase.' and everyone scattered, hooking their cans with a welding rod as they went. But I missed with my hook and had to leave the can while I hid behind the furnace. The boss walks up and stands with his hands behind his back to the furnace doors. I'm looking round the furnace and see my can begin to bubble, then glow red, then sink into one little mass of metal. Mr Chase just walked away then but he knew. Sometimes it was the highlight of the day to get past the bosses to make the tea. I've actually seen Joiners standing in a wardrobe in a ships cabin with the door shut drinking tea, 'cos if Charlie caught you with a can of tea he'd just kick it over. Then you weren't even supposed to smoke on the ship.

Then someone came up with the idea of little immersion heaters. We had 110 voltage temporary ships lights and we made a double layer wooden pad, another wooden pad for the top of your tea can with two welding rods and a bit of wire through the pad into the can. The whole thing plugged into the temporary light socket and at ten to nine every morning every light on the ship disappeared.

I got the sack for smoking once. I was doing the beamsides along an alleyway and stepped back of the block and lit up. Charlie came up and told me to go and tell my steward that he'd sacked me for smoking. Id' been working on the port side and Bob Griff, our steward, told me to take no notice of him and to go over to the starboard side and carry on with the beamsides over there. That afternoon along comes Charlie and shouts....'It's nice to see you lads working. I had to sack one of your lot on the other side this morning.' It was hard at times, it was cruel, but there was something about it, something between the men.

I used to enjoy going to work, the challenges you used to get on the ship. No two ships were ever the same and their was a big variation in the type of wood used. It was nothing to see a captains table made of bird's-eye maple and walnut with solid sliding rosewood doors. We had cases, even on the merchant boats , where once the ship was handed over we'd do little alteration to suit the crew. On one the radio officer wanted his bed to one side of his cabin, his desk the other side and the settee moving too. We did it but the inspector for the ship wouldn't accept the boat like that. We moved it back as per drawing until the ship was handed over and then put it all back again the way the radio officer wanted it.

I preferred merchant work because the standard of work was far superior. Navy work in those days was pretty plain. The Opina, Opalia and Oscilla were three tankers for Shell Oil and they were a lovely job. They all had wrought iron spiral staircases that lead to the wheelhouse and at the back, instead of ordinary panels, they had a big beautiful mural made from four 8*4 panels which had to be cut and lined up before they were fixed. That was one of the nicest jobs. Then of course, the old favourite without doubt was the Windsor Castle. We didn't have a lot to do with the big rooms. Waring and Gillows did all the first class accommodation, Heaton and Tabbs did all the tourist class work. We did the cabin work and crew work. I was first made chargehand on her.

We had some characters on the Windsor Castle. One bloke nailed up a polished panel with six inch nails right through a bulkhead. When he was told...but what about the points ? He just bent them over. We had another fella called Chalkie White, he was from Liverpool. He worked for me and all he ever did all day was to play an imaginary saxophone. I just used to throw my hands up in the air because it wasn't worth getting yourself worked up about it. You just couldn't get through to the man. We had the Tango dancer too. He came to work in a suit with his hair all slicked back, and would tango up and down the deck all day long.

In the 60's I was on a bulk carrier called the Siglion when I came across a character called Georgie Bird. He was a nice fella but wouldn't work as long as he had ears on his head. He worked for a another chargehand called George Irwin. One day George Irwin comes to look around the job to see what's been done. The answer was basically nothing. When Georgie Bird was asked why this was he replied.....'well George, in this world there's some workers and there's some idle bastards, and I'm one idle bastard.' George Irwin ended up throwing a wobbler on the aft end. What can you do with fellas like that ?

At times I've heard passing tradesmen in the yard say ...I'm not coming back here...it's like a bloody prison. Yes there was barbed wire on the walls but you still got through it. I've never regretted any of my time in Lairds. It's been good to me. I've never ever been out of work. I've never known what it's like to sign on the dole and I've been blessed with good health. We had some bad times in the yard, we had hard times, but it's been good to me. Even if someone gave us an order tomorrow, VSEL block every move that's been made. It makes me feel lousy. I had to give eight fellas their notice today. We all know it's happening and it's going to happen to me . Nothing more certain. I'm the only foreman Joiner left now.

I'd do it all again though. Lairds brought a lot of wealth to this town and they'll miss it when it shuts.What can you say about Lairds that hasn't already been said ? It's a shame. We built some of the finest ships ever and we'll build them no more.They are getting rid of the cream of shipbuilding men the like of which you'll never see again.

I think it's the thought of not being wanted that's the worst. It's the repartee at work that keeps you going. The day I get finished up I'll probably come home and then go for a walk down New Brighton prom with the wife, which we like to do. There will be days when I'm under her feet but she's probably got a list as long as your arm of jobs for me to do. I think she's looking forward to it.

It looks like the interior of a luxury cruise ship but is in fact the spiral staircase that Jack Rogers remembers on the Shell tanker Opalia,1963.

Norman Roberts

Aged 62
Boilermaker-Welder

Worked in Lairds
1954-1974

I came out of the Army and was out of work for a bit before I started at Lairds. Dad was a riveter and the chargehand boilermaker got me fixed up with a job there. I started on my first day with a fella who was an ex-SAS man... a hard man but a smashing bloke...he had a red Beret and after a while he gave me his red Beret...at least that's what he told me. Eventually he joined the police. It was like that then ..busy for a while and then bang...you are finished...out on your arse.

I started on shiprepair on piecework. I didn't have a bloody clue about piecework. I learnt myself the hard way and mixed with the welders who knew about it..You learn by experience.

The piecework at Lairds was a big con.The foremen had you by the short and curlies and could do what they liked with the book. If you had enough money in...enough to give you a decent wage...the foreman could chop you down if your face didn't fit...and you couldn't argue with a foreman.

That's the sort of thing that went on for years.

You could work bloody hard ..doing miles and miles

of footage and getting one of the lowest bills in the yard. Others...blue eyes..could do just a few feet...be on top money and also behind the book. That means they earned more than the top hourly rate allowed, I think it was 6 shillings then....only the Royals got that....they would have too much work booked in a week ...so if they were a little low a week or so later they could bring this work out that was "behind the book".

It was one big fiddle and most of the foremen were just glorified bobbies, they weren't like the foreman I'd known as an apprentice..you could respect them. Most of the foremen down there were like clockwork dolls, just wind them up and let them go.They were all frightened of the head foreman...an ex shop steward himself.

There were lighter times too on piece work, the counter-ups were the guys that would go round measuring your work. They were employed by the boilermakers union..older lads ...they'd bring them back in wheelchairs and all sorts just to give them a job...as well as measuring your work they'd do your timekeeping for you as well...there was Pat Meredith, a Rock Ferry man, he was active he was and Johnny Noonan the counter-up. Every now and again they'd come into the bays,count the work up, and then they used to do a little song and dance act... all the music hall stuff...the soft shoe shuffle and the singing...it was a regular thing, what a laugh it was..they were good though. Even if the bosses saw them they wouldn't say anything, they'd watch themselves.

You used to have happy times on shiprepair. We had some good laughs. If you get a lad whose a bit of a spinner or a storyteller you can have a good time . I was happier on repair work than new work.

In them days sacking was a normal thing. They'd tell you right away, you're sacked, finishing tonight, no two weeks notice or anything. So we'd go on the ale even though you'd only been working a few weeks. It was a normal thing although you didn't like it. You accepted it. We'd have a few pints then the parting of the ways. Sometimes you'd meet the next day and go looking for another job. More often than not you weren't on, but we tried.

Christmas time was always another time for going on the ale. Usually the Castle or the County or sometimes Green Lane..the Queens...there were a lot of pubs then. After a few pints you'd be singing and dancing, necking with the women, getting the foreman drunk and all sorts. We'd get bevied...the lads at Christmas...and I don't remember getting the turkey but I still had a turkey in my hands when I got home. Must be remote control or something.

I was made shop steward in July 1965 and the same day there was an explosion on a submarine in the North Yard, I can't remember if it was the Onyx or the Opossum. When the men had gone for their dinner there had been a build up of propane gas from a leaking propane warmer that the welders had been using...it's a heavy gas that lies on the bottom...when they went back after dinner and struck up the arc it went up like a bloody bomb. Joe McGee, a welder, had been sitting on the hatch top and it blew him right off like a bullet..he went right over the quay wall and landed on a load of old corrugated iron sheets. Alfie Baker and Barry Williams were burnt...Barry's hands were melted like bloody wax I believe and he was taken to Whiston Hospital. Joe McGee died about a week later.

I remember one time I was working on the 100 ton crane on the slipway, we had to put a new bracket or something on. Me and an erector called Reggie were in an open skip sort of thing hanging of the open hook of the crane about 200 feet up in the air. Reggie had been an erector for years ...he gets up and hold the job in position ...I welded them up. All the other erectors were standing on the crane itself watching us. Reggie jumps out of the skip and onto the crane itself....come on ..he says to me...no chance says I ...I'm going back down again this way. Then as the driver is lowering the skip back down it gets stuck against the crane....wouldn't move. So Reggie just leans out...and kicks it free...then it was swinging around like crazy about 200 feet up with me in it on my todd. Then slowly they lowered me down again.

The worst time I had was the bad weather in 1964, on a tanker on the slipway...I was on the rolling keel.I think it was the Otina...it was that cold...the coldest it had been for years...it was so cold that the steel was stuck to the ground. We couldn't do any work...they had fires everywhere trying to keep the steel warm. That's where I copped for the lumbago, the wind from the river...I was there for days.

I miss the company sometimes but not the welding. Welding's a boring repetitive job. When I look back and think about getting up in the morning and the weather we must have been maniacs to do it. Then again my great grandfather and all my family worked in Lairds and I don't want to see it shut down....it's all down to money making. Apparently somebody can make money out of the land. It shouldn't be allowed to happen. If they shut Lairds down and build on it then they can't build it up again.

The Queens Arms. Top of Green Lane and junction of Hinderton Road.

Launch of Polaris nuclear submarine HMS Renown. February 1964.

David Johnson
Aged 53
Painter

Worked in Lairds
1966-1972
1974-1993

I served my time on town work, that's private work, houses, churches, pubs and that. My dad wouldn't let me go to Lairds then because of the conditions and he wanted me to learn paperhanging as well , and you couldn't do that in Lairds. He was a Lairds painter and he knew about the conditions. He died of asbestosis through the working conditions that he tried to warn me about.

I eventually went to Lairds when I was 26 and it really was a different ball game to town work. It was dirty , noisy, dusty and not enough light, so it could be dangerous too. When I started I was put with an old hand called Ellis Parry and I went on the Spero, a car ferry.I was put in a lounge painting the portholes and windows and I thought this will do for me, this isn't too bad at all. Little did I realise. The next ship was the submarine Renown, in the reactor tunnel during the early stages. The fumes and noise were terrible and we had no lights at all. In those days the caulkers used to work next to you and the noise was very bad. You had to tell yourself that you liked it or you wouldn't last five minutes. I've seen men start at 7.30 am and go to the time office at 9.00 am for their cards because they couldn't stick it.

In those days you had to take all your gear with you. Coat, brushes, butties the lot. There weren't any huts or cabins at all, you either had your butties in the paint shop or on the boat. You can imagine what the air was like in the Paint shop so that wasn't too good. If we were on the slipways in winter we would find a cubby hole somewhere, a fix a couple of planks in it and eat our butties...we'd get a pot of shellac and burn it...it would give a little flame that lasted a long time...the only trouble was that it would make the steel bulkheads sweat and if you hung your coat up on them then they would become soaked and you went home colder than ever.

. .You didn't think it was dangerous at the time, there were gas escapes and that, and fires...you could come up from a ship and some one would say...did you see the fire in such and such a compartment?. and you didn't know anything about it.

One time on one of the Canadian Pacific boats,on the slipway,there was a tower crane built onto the aft end of the ship..it fell into the engine room cavity...of course there was no funnel or anything, just air and light.. I think the cranedriver was badly injured. To be honest, as far as we were concerned we got a whisky off the firm and were told to go into our huts..for the shock you understand ...which was fine by us of course.

When I left Lairds to go to the Water Board I knew somewhere in my heart that I would go back...not so much for the work but for the men I worked with. I used to find myself thinking , I wonder what so and so is doing now. I knew I would end up back there because of the characters that were there.

Our head foreman was George Rogers, they called him ' The Knocker 'he used to knock that many people back for jobs. One of the foreman under the Knocker was called the Dancing Master. He was a bag of nerves and used to prance about all over the place.He was terrified of the Knocker, all you had to say was ' here's the Knocker' and he'd be off like a shot. Billy Evans was another foreman who used little tricks to check up on you. He used to roll his own cigarettes and the bottom of his tobacco tin was polished up like a mirror. He'd come around with his tin and put it behind pipes and stuff and God help you if they weren't painted. On deck work he'd stand with his back to the superstructure while he was talking to you. Then behind his back he'd be rubbing his hands along the storm rail to make sure it was painted behind.We called him 'Morphia' cos he'd always say...' and when you've finished that I've got more for ya.'

When I became chargehand it was very different,.you had to do it all....planning,.supervision,.bollockings too. You were told then to go in for a foremans job and I got one. If a bollocking was required you always waited until a man was on his own or you had a private word later...never blow up at a man in front of others, and I think they appreciated that. I always had a saying.....'no see,.no book'....that's, if I don't see you I don't book you in. Some of the old arses would try it on, they would wait until they got their docket at the end of the week and then come to me and say...'Hey Dave you haven't put me in for a Saturday morning 'or whatever......

I'd say...'.but I didn't see you...'.no see...no book'

'I'll get the steward then ' they'd say

'OK then I'll go to personnel and get the police ..cos you are defrauding the company.'...

They would hum and ha but not push it...so word would go round and that sort of thing died out.

There was something about Lairds though, part of you goes out with every boat, especially a Navy boat...with all that ceremony and the men in uniforms...it always made me fill up a bit....you think of them...and we know now that some of them were in action , in the Falklands and that ...and you think of them, the crew and you somehow felt part of it.

Today I'm very bitter about what is happening to Lairds,.in a way we are responsible for our own downfall, when VSEL got hold of us we dug our own grave...we had pieces of Trident to do..on a price...and when VSEL men came to see the job they saw that the job was done as well if not better than their yard ,...and often cheaper and quicker....so we were competition.

...We were a threat...which eventually put the cat among the pigeons in Barrow...when they had to start getting their own act together.

That Noel Davies, chairman of VSEL, we call him Dole Davies, cos every time he come to Lairds he serves a HR1...the notification of redundancies,.to the dole. Now the place is being asset stripped of everything, they keep taking gear out, they say its all stuff that's been borrowed, but if you've been there a while you know what's yours and what isn't..

It's sad because we did have our bad times with strikes and that,.but now we are 100% flexible.... I will hold a pipe for a plumber,.I've even had boilermakers with a paintbrush in their hands when they were slack...they even liked it !.I'll even brush up a bit of muck around the job,..this even as a foreman is no problem now..We're a happy little crowd but getting smaller daily..We all help each other...but maybe 20 years too late.

Hitler couldn't do what is being done to us now by these people.....my dad would turn in his grave...they can kill the yard but they can't kill our pride...we were shipbuilders..and good ones too.

Polaris submarine HMS Revenge in the Mersey immediatly after her launch in March 1968.

Peter Rooney

Aged 59
Stager

Worked in Lairds
1954-1993

I had five brothers that worked in the yard. My older brother Frankie was a stager too. The first question the boss asked me was if I was afraid of heights then he asked how old I was. I knew you had to be 21, and I was only 20, so I was ready for that one, but I got it wrong and gave my correct date of birth,

'So your only 20 then son' he says, ' alright you can start but you'll only be on boys money, start Monday.'

You just were told to go with a senior stager and be put to work ..no training at all. It was all heavy work in those days, big 9*3 planks to be handled. That's why there was such a big turnover of manpower. They thought they could do the job but would pack in by dinnertime.

Luckily for me I started in good weather, it was nice , out in the open air all the time . The weather aspect of the job didn't hit me until the winter. We had some bad winters down there. Once on nights in the winter it was really bad, very ,very cold and then it started to snow. I was clearing the bases out for the staging poles. They were about six foot square at the base and set in a slide so you could move them according to the size of the ship. With the weather and the tides coming in and out they were always full of muck. You'd have no tool or anything to do it with, so you'd just use rods or any old bits of iron you could find.I was all night doing that and pulling the poles in. When I got home the next morning to go to bed I closed my eyes and I could still see the snowflakes coming at me. It was a good hour before I could get to sleep.

There was no 'it's too bad, we'll have to pack it in' you were on the job whatever. Sometimes, the weight of the planks, you'd get snow on them, trying to pick them up clean they were heavy enough, but with snow on them the weight almost doubled. We still had to clear the snow off them for the men to work on the staging. You'd get some manager coming around and telling you to turn the planks over to get rid of the snow but that made it even more hazardous as that would put all the snow and ice underneath and the staging could slide away from under a man.

In those days the discipline was very different. The Boss knew he was the Boss and kept it that way. There was no patting you on the back or anything like that. These days you can talk to a foreman or a manager but years ago they were very unapproachable and hard people. I remember one, who had no time for anything but Lairds, and had no sympathy for the sort of family problems that we all have . One night a mate of mine, Vinny Farley, didn't show up so we were a man down. He turned in the next day and explained that he'd had to take one of the kids to hospital with suspected meningitis, with a police escort...the lot. This foreman said that's no excuse and that it better not happen again. Yet the same man would buy you a pint in the ale house and could be alright, but quite unsympathetic over anything that affected the job.

Before I was married I had some good times with the Lairds lads in the ale houses around Lairds. Mondays and

Fridays were ale nights. On a Monday we'd go to the Prince Albert, knocked down now, and the Yate's at the top of Chester Road, going up towards the tunnel, and on a Friday Tom Hall's, on the Dock Road in Liverpool, at the bottom of James Street. The Red Lion too, just around the corner from James Street at the back. Used to have some good times in there. We were well known in there, never any trouble though, we just generally got bevied but there was never any fights.

It's a long day for me a Lairds, I get up at 5.15 am and get the bus to Liverpool Central at 6.10.am, get to Central about 6.45 am and the 7.05 am to Green Lane Station. I get home about 5.45 pm so I'm out of the house nearly 13 hours a day, but having said all that I don't regret working at Lairds. It's given me a good living and even though it's been hard at times I've enjoyed it.We thought of coming over this side of the water once, but nothing ever came of it so we went up to our corporation house in Speke and have been there ever since. I can't see anybody left there after July now and it's going to be a big change for me.

It's hard to visualise yourself having an extended holiday. When you do have an extended holiday it's all very nice but at the end of the day you always say you'll be glad to get back to work because you've done all the mundane stuff in the house, decorating or whatever. You're always glad to get back to work. To think now that I'm not going to work again, because at my age I've no chance, it hard to come to terms with. It's the thought of not getting up in the morning and coming out, not having the activity of coming to work and occupying my mind in work is going to be a big wrench. I'll come to terms with it but it's going to be hard.

We had our ups and downs in Lairds but it was my working life. There's always an end and this looks like the end for Lairds. Everything has an ending. There's no way out now.

Launch of the 1000th ship built at Lairds, the Clement in 1934. On the right the old style staging can be seen around the hull of another ship.

Launch of the Mauretania in 1938. The land to the south is crowded with spectators, sometimes estimated at over 100, 000 people.

Les Irwin
Aged 55
Cranedriver

Worked in Lairds
1970-1984

Before I went to Lairds I was a seaman..a ships rigger on the Harrison boats...I'd never worked in a shipyard, I didn't really know what to expect. On my first day I went into the heavy plate bay...that's where I first learnt...I always remember going there...7.30 a.m. start. Billy Robbo...he was the boss, he just said ...there you go, this fella will take you, a fella called Les Hodgie took me...he took me on the crane and I learnt from there. Later I became spare man...anyone wasn't in I was put on their crane. I didn't really like the ginny crane...once you were in you couldn't go out, you had to stay in that crane. It was interesting though, especially watching this big thing getting built and launched. When I went to see the Windsor Castle being launched I would say that I put the best part of the bow end on that in Oxo's crane.

You see it growing from the keel...and that's a ceremony all on it's own, the laying of the keel, then up through the shell, the struts and then the decks.

Every man knew the squad he was working with and that was the way it was. I was surprised to see the workings of the yard.It was so big...so many men there and yet everyone knew everyone else. It was a fantastic atmosphere.

Even then though , it wasn't as good as the mobile cranes, that was the best. It was smashing then, you could get out and have a bit of a chat with the lads, do a bit of slinging and then get back in. You travelled all around the yard doing different jobs.

We had a really good bunch of men there...a good squad, we had a few drinks too. Every night the cranedrivers would have a drink after work. All over to the Castle you know.

I remember one time when a cranedriver died. Lets say his name was George...George died on his crane, the 15 tonner on the basin. Whenever anything like that happened there would be a canvas collection...somebody would throw a big tarpaulin on the ground by the gate on paynight and all hands would throw money onto it. We would always have the time off for the funeral and there would be a chara laid on to take us to Landican Cemetery. So we buried George. Then coming back on the chara and someone said

"Let's go in the Lord Raglen for a pint ."

So the driver says." You can't , I've got to get you back!"

So we all told him we had to go to the toilet, so we got off and were all in the Raglen drinking.

The next thing the phone rings.

It was Billy Robbo, foreman cranedriver,

"Any cranedrivers in there" he says, " this is Billy Robbo...tell them I want them all back at work now."

One of the lads shouted back..."Tell him he's got more chance of George coming back!"

Some people think that because you are out of the way they couldn't check on you as much, but every morning we had to be in early to do our greasing...what we had to do at night was take our hook right up top limit..that way Robbo would know your crane was unmanned ..but in the morning we had to lower off...and that told him that you were in. It was the only way they could do it, there were so many cranes over such a huge area. Then he would know where he needed his spare men.

The money wasn't that good on a flat week but you got a lot of overtime...that was the thing for us. When you were on a busy ship you could get a lot of hours in..nights as well.

When I started , there were about 80 cranedrivers...I think there's about three now. All in all it was the longest job I ever stuck, more than at sea and in Fords. I think I stayed so long because of the atmosphere of the place. All the blokes, everyone you seemed to work with was great. All good men. All knew their job. It was a fine, fine shipyard.

The Lord Raglen Hotel, bottom of Union Street, Birkenhead.

Maureen Mallon

Aged Over 21
Occupational Health
Nurse

Worked in Lairds
1988-1993

Before I worked at Cammell Lairds I didn't know about the yard at all. I'm originally from West Kirby and believe it or not I was completely oblivious to the name of Cammell Laird. I'd never heard of them, and yet, at the time I was working in Arrowe Park Hospital. I'd never even been there to see a ship launched when I was a schoolgirl. It was such a shock for me when I went to Cammell Lairds. I thought the place was so dirty and I was just totally and utterly disgusted. I was introduced to everybody, and they took me around the shipyard and I thought the men are so dirty, they were just so dirty.

The first time I went onto a ship was the submarine HMS Unseen. They didn't have a boiler suit or anything to fit me and when I was going aboard I happened to look back and there were all these men looking up my dress. Never again, but then when I saw the inside of the submarine , how small and cramped everything was I couldn't believe it..., how did anyone ever manage to work in such conditions ? Then I started to wonder how on earth I could ever get anyone out of such a place in the event of an emergency. So later on we set up a mock evacuation of a casualty out of the submarine. I think that's when the men could see that I was trying to do something for them and started to accept me a little more.

When I was in the Army I had rank, which is irrelevant for a nurse as you just push that apart and it didn't matter whether you were dealing with the lowest soldier or a Major. The only difference was the colour of their curtains or if they had a carpet or not. Cammell Lairds is no different, from a plumber to a manager. The difference in Lairds is the humour of the men there, you're a 'love' there, or a 'Hey Love' or 'Hey Mo'. You have to earn your respect from a plater or a caulker, you take that bit out of his eye and he'll come back again.

If there is something in a mans eye we say we think it's about 3 o'clock or 7 o'clock or whatever, but one man, Davy Dunn, would come in and say...'It's about 12 o'clock' and he was always spot on.

It was a similar story when people would get a flash from the welding arc. The men used to come in before they went home and say..'give us a couple of those drops love...I've got a flash'. They knew that they were going to wake up in the middle of the night with it. They were usually right. The company still have a policy that if a man gets a flash he can have the next day off as long as they visit the surgery. I'd say we had a few who were playing the game but in the main they were very genuine.

The first major incident I was involved in was when an electrician in the construction hall was hit by a load on a crane. He had bad internal injuries, was bleeding from them, and a fractured spine. I evacuated him and wait until the paramedics arrived .

Later on I was back in the surgery refilling my bags and equipment when the call came through that the man who had been driving the crane at the time had suffered a heart attack and was still in his crane. The Safety man I was with was not too keen on heights and so I had to go all the way up alone ...along the top, into the crane, along the jib and into the little cabin space. The driver was there slumped over his drivers chair. By this time the Fire Service and the police had arrived and were all staring up at us in this little cabin. The crane driver kept saying....'I've killed him, I've killed him haven't I ?

I told him that he hadn't and he said his legs wouldn't move. So we had a cigarette together , but because I'd left my radio at the other end of the crane I couldn't tell anyone that he was O.K. So we had our cigarette and then he managed to move his legs and we got him down. He went off for a while then with shock.

These men that had been treated for one thing or another often came back to the surgery with all sorts of different things that they had made in the yard, that they thought I could use at home. They'd bring me an iron grillwork type of mat and say....'that's for your front door.' All sorts of things....plant pot holders...big steel markers to stick in the front garden with my house number on...that fruit bowl over there...the window box out there...just anything and everything. That's when I found out what 'foreigners' were. The funny thing is that I never asked for any of these things , they just arrived, like the three kings!

What it brought home to me was that these men could make just about anything and I was amazed, and still am, that they can do that. The first time I saw a ship launched I suppose I actually felt proud of knowing the men that had put it together, because I really don't know much about how ships are built and things like that. I felt like part of the family then , accepted. I know nearly all of the men now and feel part of it.

I feel sure that the place won't close, even now, and I'm

the only one that thinks so. I must stay positive about it because the men know I feel that way so in a way I suppose it keeps their spirits up a bit.So much so that I wrote to the Queen about it to see if we could be considered to build a replacement for the Royal Yacht Brittannia. Unfortunately she didn't write back as it was passed on to the Ministry of Defence. They just said that it was out of their hands really. I wrote to Michael Heseltine too. I told him I didn't know anything about shipping or about politics..I just said help us.But they just wrote back and said it was a private company and that the government don't intervene in private companies.

I took my son to see the last launch, it was his first time and he was very excited , he really was. It was absolutely,desperately sad. Why won't there be any more ? I don't know whose to blame but it isn't Cammell Laird, everyone that you talk to about it says that Cammell Lairds do a really good job. It's all damn political. The politicians are saying it's a private company but I tend to listen to the men in the yard. I think everything has been mapped out a long time ago. You've served your purpose now...thanks very much.

It will be heartbreaking if it goes. It's the end of a huge cosmopolitan family. I can't really, in my heart, admit that it's going to close.

Miss A Mallon
Cammell Laird Shipbuilders Ltd
New Chester Road
Birkenhead
L41 9BP

Department of Trade and Industry

Buckingham Palace Road
London SW1W 9SS

Enquiries
071-215 5000

Telex 8813148 DIHQ G
Fax 071-215 2909

071-215 1135
SP/GEN/56B

26 February 1993

Dear Miss Mallon

I have been asked by the President of the Board of Trade to
reply to your letter of 9 February 1993 on the closure of the
Cammell Laird shipyard.

The Government were sorry to hear that the parent company of
Cammell Laird, Vickers Shipbuilding and Engineering Limited
(VSEL), had been unable to find a buyer for the Cammell Laird
shipyard and that the shipyard is to close. This is a
commercial decision on the part of VSEL, and since Cammell
Laird is a private company it would be wrong for the
Government to directly intervene. However, I can assure you
that our regional staff are fully aware of the situation and
are currently involved with proposals to create new investment
and safeguard jobs in the Birkenhead area. Hopefully some of
these proposals will be successful and turn into active
projects, providing new opportunities for the workers from
Cammell Laird.

Yours sincerely

MIKE CURTIS
Shipbuilding Unit
Vehicles Division

3STFTK.051

dti
the department for Enterprise

*Reply to Maureen Mallon's letter to Michael Heseltine asking for help
for the yard.*

101

From: Jenny Speirs, Resources and Programmes (Navy) 2

Ms M Mallon
Cammell Laird Shipbuilders Ltd
New Chester Road   D/RP(N)118/1/2
Birkenhead
L41 9BP   18 March 1993

Dear Ms Mallon

    Thank you for your letter of 5 February to Her Majesty The Queen, about the contract for a new Royal Yacht. Your letter has been passed to the Ministry of Defence for reply as we are the Government Department responsible for the Royal Yacht.

    You asked in your letter if any contract for a new Royal Yacht could be awarded to Cammell Laird and it might be helpful if I set out the current position with regard to the future of the Royal Yacht. In view of her age, we are currently considering HMY BRITANNIA's future. However, this consideration is at an early stage and it is too early to speculate on the outcome.

    The Government is fully aware of the importance of defence equipment contracts to industry, and we recognise that Cammell Laird have built many fine ships over the years. However, even if a decision had been taken to order a new Royal Yacht and, as I have outlined above we are not in that position, it is Government policy that contracts are awarded on the basis of competition following full evaluation of tenders and we could, therefore, make no guarantee to place a contract with any particular company.

    I am sorry that I cannot be more helpful.

Yours Sincerely

Jenny Speirs

Reply, from Ministry of Defence, to Maureen's letter to the Queen, which is self explanatory.

102

Albert Richards

Aged 76
Brassfinisher

Worked in Lairds
1932-1945

I used to work on the railway dining cars as a young lad and I liked that too , then when I got finished up I was lucky that I knew someone who got me in Lairds as a tradesman. I only ended up in Lairds because there was no other work about at the time. I didn't choose it, my parents more or less did that. They said they'd seen someone called Arthur George, a foreman in the engine shop and there was a job there if I wanted one. I had to go .We had a big family, and I had to start working.

I didn't have a clue about what Cammell Lairds was never mind anything else. I'd worked on railway dining cars, never a shipyard. I was just a kid. Everything there was dirty and scruffy, but I learnt it.

A Brassfinisher was a sort of fitter turner.He did all the brass work, a bit of welding...everything to do with brass in the big ships. Brass, copper, zinc, gunmetal and that. We had to learn how to braze too, metals that were a bit out of the ordinary.

On the railways I was getting about 11 bob a week plus 3 bob out of my lodging allowance which was 14 bob. When I went to Lairds I was on 8 shillings a week. That was my wages. Out of that they docked sixpence for my indentures and after insurance and that I got roughly 6 shillings or 6 shillings and a penny each week. You had to buy you own overalls and shoes and everything yourself, a pair of overalls was about 5 shillings and sixpence then in Lewis's. My mother and father had a big family and nothing else, they had to pay for me to serve my time, I don't know how much.

Lairds was like a bloody prison. I was used to being outside. I loved being outside and I was just dragged into Lairds and that was it.

There's a place called the Pyramids now in downtown Birkenhead. Where that is used to be a place called Stafford Street where we lived. A little two bedroom house with two rooms downstairs. We had a Donkey's breakfast, a straw mattress that was carted upstairs during the day and brought down at night and put on two chairs and I slept on that, a Donkey's breakfast. The old seamen brought them out and I slept on that for years.

We made a bit of extra money from bringing brass and that out of the yard. When the old Rodney went out, she was the main one, a battleship that went out about 1928. After that there was loads of spare gear left, gunmetal and that...I was drawn in with all the fellas that did that and we'd take it over the road to the scrappies yard and get 2 shillings for it. I've walked out of that gate with nearly my own weight in brass and stuff. We weren't the only ones, there were loads. You even got fined for smoking then. I was fined at least four times. Two shillings and sixpence each time..no joke... and I had to go home and tell my father that I'd been fined for smoking. During my time, I got caught taking gear out. I got suspended for three weeks and when I came back they said they should be sacking me and it could affect my indentures money. I didn't give a damn and so that was that.

I came out of my time and got my indentures money...two pounds. Six of use went on the ale, over to the Castle, and we soon got through the two quid.

I almost had my hand taken off once when I'd just come out of my time. I was on the circular saw. My hand was caught in it and I was off work for 18 weeks. All I got was what they called then workmans compensation. That was 2/3rds of the money you were earning at the time. Then I was on about 9 shillings so I got about 6 shillings a week. The scars are still there now.

I tried to get out of Lairds to go away to sea but I was caught by the war so there was no chance of getting out so I went right through the war there. I was shit scared sometimes, in Lairds and in the town when there was a raid on. I remember running like hell from one side of the slipway to the other to the shelter such as it was. When we got out someone said ...he's hit the Prince of Wales. When we went to see her the fire service was there and there she was, keeling over. Down below one of her storm valves or something had been blown out as the bomb had gone between her and the quay wall, and the water just flooded in.

The Achilles was a cracker of a ship. She was a beauty, a cruiser. She was the first one that you could say was a beautiful little ship.I think she was the first one to have 3.7" guns on but I'm not sure. I remember the Thetis too. We didn't realise, all we knew was that she'd gone on trials..then we heard that she'd gone down and was on the bottom. We all worked like hell then to get something out there as quick as we could, there was a ship called the Zelo and we fastened huge great wooden keel blocks to her sides. The idea was to fasten the tail end of the Thetis to the Zelo and when the tide went down the Zelo would pull the sub out. So everybody worked.

That was supposed to be the rescue, but she was flying the White Ensign at the time and the Admiralty had taken her over.They said they would do things their way and that they had a man coming from London to oversee the job...so they missed two or three tides. It was a bloody disgrace.

My only regret about being in Lairds was going there in the first place and being stuck there for all those years. To me it was like a bloody life sentence.

HMS Rodney in the Mersey circa 1928. She was in service long enough to participate in the sinking of the Bismark during World War Two.

Launch of the ill fated submarine Thetis in 1939. Lost on sea trials in the same year, taking 99 souls with her, many of them Lairdsmen.

Charlie Campbell
Aged 53
Blacksmith

Worked in Lairds
1956-1993

The conditions the thing that I really remember when I first started. In the Smithy there was loads of smoke and a horrible smell of sulphur from the burning coke. The dirt. It was a dirt floor, there was no concrete on the floor, because of the vibration from the hammers. I hated it at first. I didn't like the muck and I didn't like the job itself. It was a horrible job.

An uncle of mine was a Black and he'd got me a start. I came straight from school and never heard of a Blacksmith. I was introduced to the other lads in the shop. They were the hammer lads. The name's a little misleading because hammer lads were anything from 15 to 80, there was a lot of old hammer lads and the first job you learn is how to drive the hammer. They were steam driven in the winter and wind in the summer.

They had a safety, it was called a kicker...a bar connected to a handle and as the head of the hammer came up if you came up too high with it, it hit the kicker which was spring loaded and it would push your hand back down again and that would bring the hammer down. Depending on how hard the kicker was hit you could keep hold of it but if it hit too hard it would fly out of your hand and then it would be every man for himself. That was the kind of thing you were doing from day one.

You used to sit alongside the hammer and a more experienced 'lad' would stand behind you holding your hand until you got the rhythm of the hammer going up and down. The Blacksmith would be nodding his head if he wanted you to hit harder and the other striker would be shouting 'go on' and you could get mixed up but you got it in the end.

You learned how to strike, all the tools, the tongs, the different formers and all the rest of it, anvil tools, hammer tools. When you went into the Smithy you'd see like a mound of scrap...they were all the tools. People used to ask me how we ever found anything in there but the blacksmith knew every tool that was in that mound. You had to learn them all too and learn how to strike left handed. That's how it went see. hammer lad, striker, Blacksmith.

The Blacksmith would stand so that if you swung the hammer right-handed you'd connect with his head, so you had to swing left-handed...to perfect the technique it was hitting yourself on the shin. Once you'd missed everything else and hit yourself on the shin you never missed anything again.

The men you were working for, the black and the striker, they were your boss, not the boss in the office. They told you when you started, when you had your break, and when you knocked off. If you messed around, and all lads mess around, they'd clip you around the ear and they were all big strong men. Old Sidney Swan had a massive mate, George Carter, a big strong strapping fella. If you said which one's the Blacksmith you'd say the big strapping one, but little Sid was the Blacksmith. They were like Little and Large.

At the same time it was piecework so they couldn't afford to let you mess around. When the bars went into the fire you started and you stopped when the bars ran out. If you had a load of bars in you might work through with no break. Not for your benefit because you still got apprentices money...£2.5s (£2.20p) a week. I got the 5 shillings my mum had the £2. If you worked like that his money would go up...whatever work they put out the money went up. When it was my turn to get some extra money it all used to go in the 'back of the book'. We never got any more money and when we had a bit of a moan they'd say..It's in the back of the book son...when your a bit short you'll be alright. You got the same wages every week ...they just kidded you.

There were lots of disabled fellas in the Smithy too. I remember John Carter...he had no legs. He was a hammer lad. Eventually he was fitted with legs...they didn't have straps, they had like a valve that had like a stocking in it. When you pulled the stocking thing out of the valve it caused a vacuum which made the leg stick to his stumps. He used to drive a Morris Minor with hand controls, but if he caught his knee on the door getting out the vacuum would go and his leg would drop off. Then he'd be stuck in the car until someone came to get him out.

The Smithy was split up into three or four different graded fires. If you were on a small fire, small hammer, you'd get the least wages and so on. Bigger fires did more technical work, more responsibility and your wages went up. Eventually you got to the big fire...they would make anything , out of old propeller shafts. They had an old hammer lad there, Paddy Miller he was about 82. He was a Blacksmith, lost his fingers, he only had his little finger and thumb...he chewed tobacco and used to drive the big hammer. When he retired he was on the television walking down what we used to call 'Smithy Road' outside the shop and we were all waving to him.

Your ambition was always to get on to the big fire, but they closed the Smithy down before I ever made it.

By the time the Smithy was closed down eventually I had I started outside on the ships to get more experience, it stood me in good stead in the end. I think the first one was the Devonshire. I remember one ship that I couldn't wait to get off the job..it was a tanker, the British Ensign. There was a fore and aft gangway on it that seemed to go on for miles every time you did something to it, it seemed to twist..trying to keep that job plumb and square was murder.

Later, on the CP boats, we had to do a job on the masthead..we had a welder with us, everybody called him 'Friggin' Albert...every other word was 'friggin'.

He said..."I'm not going up the friggin mast.."..

I said "Well, we've got a Bosun's chair to go up in."

"I wouldn't go up there in a friggin three piece suite!" he said.

Most people these days don't know I'm a Blacksmith , I'm the last one there. Because I work mostly with Shipwrights now they think I am too. They use to say 'where're the horses' or 'Can you nail a shoe on a horse?' I'd say...well you get it on it's back and I'll nail a shoe on it!

We don't have a fire now, ...if I need any warming we use propane or acetylene gas and oxygen. I still use some of the tools and formers that I keep in my box, some of them have got peoples initials on them...they must be 100 years old. All the hammers were just smashed up in the end except a little one ton hammer that went to the Millwrights shop.

I loved every minute that I was in Lairds. I still do now. You forget the bad times. As the years have gone by the conditions have got easier. There's a lot of fellas have gone...I've seen them crying. I just hope it doesn't happen to me as I can get a bit emotional like that. I don't work with anybody really closely. I come into contact with a lot of people but I don't have a lot of people around me. Some of these lads have worked with each other since they were 15...I've seen them ...going out at 63 years of age, crying, because that's the end. Unless they keep in touch with each other, going out of them gates is the last time they're going to see each other.

I know my time for the OBE is coming soon, and when it does my face will hit the floor. I'll feel like I've had my hands cut off. I don't know what went wrong. If I was clever enough I'd have to blame the management. I've no axe to grind but there's no way you could blame the workmen. The way it is now Vickers have taken everything out of the yard...all the level beds, keel blocks, the lot...everything you need to build a ship. I feel sorry about what's going to happen to the country, what's going to happen for my grandkids...what kind of society...will they ever have a job when it's their time?

It's finding something to do. I'll probably drive my missis round the bend.

Charlie Campbell was probably the most modest man I have ever met in my life. During the course of our interview Charlies wife pointed out his photograph in a Cammell Laird Magazine of the 1960s wearing a Judo suit. Charlie was British Lightweight Judo Champion more than once and also achieved an Olympic trial in this sport. He has taught Judo to youngsters for more than 30 years. Charlie did not talk about this work or his achievements during our time together.

Charlie, like many others, was made redundant from Cammell Laird in April 1993.

WDR

The tanker British Ensign being pulled into the Wet Basin in 1963. Charlie Cambell remembers the difficult job on the fore and aft walkway of this huge 70, 000 ship

Charlie Campbell, with the hat, as a young man in the Blacksmiths Shop. The old steam hammer and anvil can just about be seen.

A BRIEF GLOSSARY OF SHIPYARD TERMS

D.C.M / O.B.E

..... The sack, made redundant, finished up.."Don't come Monday."or the "Old Brown Envelope."

Over the wall

....Out of the yard when you should be in the yard...still on pay but not at work.

The Bank

....The slipways...out in the open on the early stages of building a ship.

The Basin

The wet basin or dock, where a ship is now afloat after launching but where there is still all the fitting out work, accommodation ,engines etc. to be done.

Caisson

A floating gate , often with their own small engines, that were used as the gates between a dry dock and the river.

Ginny Crane

A gantry crane with a small lifting capacity, usually inside a workshop.

A Flash

A common, but very painful burning sensation in the eye caused by being exposed to the flash of a welding arc.

Slinger

A worker responsible for the correct and safe positioning of lifting slings around a load to be lifted.

Gash

Spare, going begging, not in use.

Cockwood

Old bits of wood taken home for the fire. This would keep the wives at home happy.

A 'day out' or 'docked half a day'

A day off, sick, or just didn't get up in time. This would result in the loss of a day or half a days pay.

Over the Water

Liverpool is referred to as 'over the water' from Birkenhead and vice versa.

Royals

Favoured workers who were given the best paying jobs to do.

Brightening the Lines

Steel plates would be marked by the Platers using a chalk line and a pop marker, making lines on the steel like ruling lines on paper. Over time these chalked lines would fade and need 'brightening' by re-chalking.

Scriber

A sharply pointed hardened steel marking tool for marking out steel plates.

Cantilevers

A high crane of the sort of construction as on the front cover of this book. Usually has a fixed base.

Staging Pull

One row or column of staging boards around a ship.

Foreigners

Jobs for home and house. Take home jobs using Lairds's materials, and time.

Slew, Rack out, Block

The block is that part of the crane that carries the main cables and hook. This is suspended by a trolley that racks in and out along the main horizontal structure of the crane. This structure could slew or rotate around the fixed vertical crane structure.

Busbars

A bar , usually copper, that serves as a common electrical connector for several pieces of electrical equipment.

Gennies

Electricity generators

A Butt

A welded joint where the pieces to be welded are not overlapped but fitted directly next to each other.

A Bill

The weekly total of a mans earnings on piecework. Always a subject of serious negotiations.

A 'Chara'

What we would call today a coach, a motor coach. Slang for a charabanc.

The White Ensign

The flag of the British Royal Navy. Only Naval vessels are permitted to fly this ensign.

LIST OF ROYAL NAVY VESSELS BUILT BY CAMMELL LAIRD.

Ship No.	Name	Type	Build Year
31	DOVER	MAIL PACKET	1840
34	SOUDAN	GUNBOAT	1840
35	ALBERT	GUNBOAT	1840
36	WIBERFORCE	GUNBOAT	1840
51	BIRKENHEAD	FRIGATE	1846
115	RESOLUTE	TROOPSHIP	1855
116	ASSISTANCE	TROOPSHIP	1855
129	THAIS	DESPATCH SHIP	1855
132	SIREN	DESPATCH SHIP	1855
151	BEACON	GUNBOAT	1856
152	BRAVE	GUNBOAT	1856
153	BULLFINCH	GUNBOAT	1856
154	REDBREST	GUNBOAT	1856
155	ROSE	GUNBOAT	1856
156	BLAZER	GUNBOAT	1856
157	RAINBOW	GUNBOAT	1856
158	BRAZEN	GUNBOAT	1856
159	RAVEN	GUNBOAT	1856
160	ROCKET	GUNBOAT	1856
161	CUPID	MORTER BOAT	1855
162	BLOSSOM	GUNBOAT	1856
163	GADFLY	GUNBOAT	1856
164	GNAT	GUNBOAT	1856
165	GARLAND	GUNBOAT	1856
179	UNAMED	MORTER BOAT	1856
180	UNAMED	MORTER BOAT	1856
181	UNAMED	MORTER BOAT	1856
182	UNAMED	MORTER BOAT	1856
183	UNAMED	MORTER BOAT	1856
184	UNAMED	MORTER BOAT	1856
185	UNAMED	MORTER BOAT	1856
186	UNAMED	MORTER BOAT	1856
187	UNAMED	MORTER BOAT	1856
188	UNAMED	MORTER BOAT	1856
189	UNAMED	MORTER BOAT	1856
190	UNAMED	MORTER BOAT	1856

191	UNAMED	MORTER BOAT	1856
193	UNAMED	MORTER BOAT	1856
274	CHESTER	TANK BOAT	1861
286	ORONTES T	ROOP SHIP	1862
291	AGINCOURT	ARMOUR CLAD	1865
294	SCORPION	ARMOUR CLAD	1863
295	WIVERN	ARMOUR CLAD	1863
322	L	LAUNCH	1865
325	EUPHRATES	TROOP SHIP	1866
346	CAPTAIN	ARMOUR CLAD	1869
362	TEAZER	GUNBOAT	1868
366	VANGUARD	BATTLESHIP	1869
434	GRIFFON	GUNBOAT	1876
435	FALCON	GUNBOAT	1877
438	SAMPSON	TUG	1877
493	CLIVE	TROOP SHIP	1882
506	ALBACORE	SLOOP	1883
507	MISTLETOE	SLOOP	1883
508	WATCHFUL	SLOOP	1883
517	ETNA	TUG	1883
518	METEOR	TUG	1883
537	RATTLESNAKE	TORPEDO BOAT	1886
579	ROYAL OAK	BATTLESHIP	1892
585	ONYX	TORPEDO GUNBOAT	1892
586	RENARD	TORPEDO GUNBOAT	1892
591	NO-97	TORPEDO BOAT	1893
596	FERRET	TB DESTROYER	1893
597	LYNX	TB DESTROYER	1894
598	BANSHEE	TB DESTROYER	1894
599	CONTEST	TB DESTROYER	1894
600	DRAGON	TB DESTROYER	1894
603	MARS	BATTLESHIP	1896
606	QUAIL	TB DESTROYER	1895
607	SPARROWHAWK	TB DESTROYER	1895
608	THRASHER	TB DESTROYER	1895
609	VIRAGO	TB DESTROYER	1895
621	ERNEST	TB DESTROYER	1896
622	GRIFFON	TB DESTROYER	1896
623	LOCUST	TB DESTROYER	1896
624	PANTHER	TB DESTROYER	1897

625	SEAL	TB DESTROYER	1897
626	WOLF	TB DESTROYER	1897
629	EXPRESS	TB DESTROYER	1897
630	GLORY	BATTLESHIP	1899
633	ORWELL	TB DESTROYER	1898
635	MUTINE	SLOOP	1900
636	RINALDO	SLOOP	1900
638	EXMOUTH	BATTLESHIP	1901
639	LIVELY	TB DESTROYER	1900
640	SPRIGHTLY	TB DESTROYER	1900
649	FOYLE	TB DESTROYER	1903
650	ITCHER	TB DESTROYER	1903
651	ARUN	TB DESTROYER	1903
652	BLACKWATER	TB DESTROYER	1903
653	TOPAZE	CRUISER	1903
654	DIAMOND	CRUISER	1904
655	PATHFINDER	SCOUT VESSEL	1904
658	PATROL	SCOUT VESSEL	1904
659	LIFFEY	TB DESTROYER	1904
660	MOY	TB DESTROYER	1904
661	OUSE	TB DESTROYER	1905
663	TEST	TB DESTROYER	1905
664	STOUR	TB DESTROYER	1905
667	COSSACK	TB DESTROYER	1907
671	SWIFT	TB DESTROYER	1907
691	RENARD	TB DESTROYER	1909
692	WOLVERINE	TB DESTROYER	1910
693	RACOON	TB DESTROYER	1910
713	LAPWING	TB DESTROYER	1911
714	LIZARD	TB DESTROYER	1911
720	ADAMANT	TENDER	1911
721	ALECTO	TENDER	1911
728	HB	HORSE BOAT	1908
770	FD	FLOATING DOCK	1912
772	MELBOURNE	CRUISER	1912
775	AUDACIUOS	BATTLESHIP	1912
786	GARLAND	TB DESTROYER	1913
803	CAROLINE	LIGHT CRUISER	1914
809	BIRKENHEAD	CRUISER	1915
810	KEMPENFELT	TB DESTROYER	1915

811	CHESTER	CRUISER	1916
812	CASTOR	LIGHT CRUISER	1915
813	CONSTANCE	LIGHT CRUISER	1916
814	E41	SUBMARINE	1916
815	E42	SUBMARINE	1916
816	E45	SUBMARINE	1916
817	E46	SUBMARINE	1916
818	GABRIEL	DESTROYER	1916
819	ITHURIEL	DESTROYER	1916
820	ABDIEL	MINELAYER	1916
822	PARKER	FLOTTILLA LEADER	1916
823	GRENVILLE	FLOTTILLA LEADER	1916
824	HOSTE	FLOTTILLA LEADER	1916
825	SEYMOUR	FLOTTILLA LEADER	1916
826	SAUMAREZ	FLOTTILLA LEADER	1916
828	CALEDON	LIGHT CRUISER	1917
829	VALENTINE	FLOTTILLA LEADER	1917
830	VALHALLA	FLOTTILLA LEADER	1917
831	SCOTT	FLOTTILLA LEADER	1918
832	L7	SUBMARINE	1917
833	L8	SUBMARINE	1918
827	BRUCE	FLOTTILLA LEADER	1918
838	DOUGLAS	FLOTTILLA LEADER	1918
849	CAMPBELL	DESTROYER	1918
850	MACKAY	DESTROYER	1919
851	MALCOLM	DESTROYER	1919
870	CAIRO	LIGHT CRUISER	1919
871	CAPETOWN	LIGHT CRUISER	1919
872	H33	SUBMARINE	1919
873	H34	SUBMARINE	1919
877	R12	SUBMARINE	1918
904	RODNEY	BATTLESHIP	1927
941	PHOENIX	SUBMARINE	1931
983	ACHILLES	CRUISER	1933
989	SEALION	SUBMARINE	1934
990	SALMON	SUBMARINE	1935
992	FEARLESS	DESTROYER	1934
993	FORESIGHT	DESTROYER	1935
1008	HARDY	FLOTTILLA LEADER	1936
1011	SPEARFISH	SUBMARINE	1936

1012	ARK ROYAL	AIRCRAFT CARRIER	1938
1015	INGLEFIELD	FLOTILLA LEADER	1937
1026	PRINCE OF WALES	BATTLESHIP	1941
1027	THETIS	SUBMARINE	1939
1028	TRIDENT	SUBMARINE	1939
1033	DIDO	CRUISER	1940
1036	TAKU	SUBMARINE	1940
1038	GURKHA	DESTROYER	1941
1039	LIVELY	DESTROYER	1941
1040	TALISMAN	SUBMARINE	1940
1041	CHARYBOIS	CRUISER	1941
1043	ATHERSTONE	ESCORT VESSEL	1940
1044	BERKELEY	ESCORT VESSEL	1940
1047	ARGONAUT	CRUISER	1941
1048	BLENCATHRA	ESCORT VESSEL	1940
1049	BROCKLESBY	ESCORT VESSEL	1941
1050	THRASHER	SUBMARINE	1941
1051	THORN	SUBMARINE	1941
1052	TEMPEST	SUBMARINE	1941
1055	BADSWORTH	ESCORT VESSEL	1941
1056	BEAUFORT	ESCORT VESSEL	1941
1057	SAFARI	SUBMARINE	1942
1058	SAHIB	SUBMARINE	1942
1059	SARACEN	SUBMARINE	1942
1062	SYBIL	SUBMARINE	1942
1063	SEADOG	SUBMARINE	1942
1064	RAIDER	DESTROYER	1942
1065	RAPID	DESTROYER	1943
1069	ML	MOTOR BOAT	1940
1070	ML	MOTOR BOAT	1940
1071	ML	MOTOR BOAT	1940
1072	ML	MOTOR BOAT	1941
1073	ML	MOTOR BOAT	1940
1074	ML	MOTOR BOAT	1941
1075	ML	MOTOR BOAT	1941
1076	ML	MOTOR BOAT	1941
1077	ALDENHAM	DESTROYER	1942
1078	BELVOIR	DESTROYER	1942
1079	TLC5	TANK LANDING CRAFT	1940
1080	TLC6	TANK LANDING CRAFT	1940

1081	GLAISDALE	DESTROYER	1942
1082	ESKDALE	DESTROYER	1942
1083	SEA NYMPH	SUBMARINE	1942
1084	SICKLE	SUBMARINE	1942
1085	SIMOON	SUBMARINE	1942
1086	131	MOTOR LAUNCH	1941
1087	132	MOTOR LAUNCH	1941
1088	133	MOTOR LAUNCH	1941
1089	134	MOTOR LAUNCH	1941
1090	TLC 23	TANK LANDING CRAFT	1941
1091	TLC 24	TANK LANDING CRAFT	1941
1092	TLC 111	TANK LANDING CRAFT	1941
1093	TLC 112	TANK LANDING CRAFT	1941
1094	SCORPION	DESTROYER	1943
1095	SCOURGE	DESTROYER	1943
1096	STUBBORN	SUBMARINE	1943
1097	SURF	SUBMARINE	1943
1098	SYRTIS	SUBMARINE	1943
1099	TEAZER	DESTROYER	1943
1100	TENACIOUS	DESTROYER	1943
1101	CYGNET	SLOOP	1942
1102	KITE	SLOOP	1943
1103	ULYSSES	DESTROYER	1943
1104	UNDAUNTED	DESTROYER	1944
1106	EMPIRE MACOLL	MERCHANT A/C	1943
1107	STOIC	SUBMARINE	1943
1108	STONEHENGE	SUBMARINE	1943
1109	STORM	SUBMARINE	1943
1110	STRATAGEM	SUBMARINE	1943
1111	SALVEDA	SALVAGE VESSEL	1943
1114	SPIRIT	SUBMARINE	1943
1115	STATESMAN	SUBMARINE	1943
1117	ZAMBESI	DESTROYER	1944
1118	ZEALOUS	DESTROYER	1944
1119	ARK ROYAL	AIRCRAFT CARRIER	1955
1122	STURDY	SUBMARINE	1943
1123	STYGIAN	SUBMARINE	1944
1124	HOGUE	FLEET DESTROYER	1945
1125	LAGOS	FLEET DESTROYER	1945
1126	VENERABLE	AIRCRAFT CARRIER	1945

1127	GRAVELINES	FLEET DESTROYER	1946
1128	SLUYS	FLEET DESTROYER	1946
1129	SUBTLE	SUBMARINE	1944
1130	SUPREME	SUBMARINE	1944
1131	SEASCOUT	SUBMARINE	1944
1132	SELENE	SUBMARINE	1944
1134	SOLENT	SUBMARINE	1944
1135	SLEUTH	SUBMARINE	1944
1136	SIDON	SUBMARINE	1944
1137	SPEARHEAD	SUBMARINE	1944
1138	SPUR	SUBMARINE	1945
1139	SCORCHER	SUBMARINE	1945
1140	SANGUINE	SUBMARINE	1945
1141	SAGA	SUBMARINE	1945
1142	SPRINGER	SUBMARINE	1945
1143	AFFRAY	SUBMARINE	1946
1144	AENEAS	SUBMARINE	1946
1145	ALARIC	SUBMARINE	1946
1161	LCT 7043	LANDING CRAFT	1944
1162	LCT 7044	LANDING CRAFT	1944
1163	LCT 7045	LANDING CRAFT	1944
1164	LCT 7046	LANDING CRAFT	1944
1165	LCT 7047	LANDING CRAFT	1944
1166	LCT 7048	LANDING CRAFT	1944
1167	LCT 49	LANDING CRAFT	1944
1168	LCT 50	LANDING CRAFT	1944
1229	WHITBY	FRIGATE	1956
1233	TENBY	FRIGATE	1957
1238	GRAMPUS	SUBMARINE	1959
1239	FINWHALE	SUBMARINE	1960
1265	SEALION	SUBMARINE	1961
1284	DEVONSHIRE	G/MISSILE DESTROYER	1962
1285	AJAX	FRIGATE	1963
1288	ODIN	SUBMARINE	1962
1297	ORACLE	SUBMARINE	1963
1306	OPOSSUM	SUBMARINE	1963
1310	MANDARIN	SALVAGE VESSEL	1964
1311	PINTAIL	SALVAGE VESSEL	1964
1316	RENOWN	POLARIS SUBMARINE	1969
1317	REVENGE	POLARIS SUBMARINE	1969

1319	ONYX	SUBMARINE	1967
1330	CONQUEROR	NUCLEAR SUBMARINE	1971
1308	BIRMINGHAM	T42 DESTROYER	1976
1309	COVENTRY	T42 DESTROYER	1978
1366	BAYLEAF	R.F.AUXILIARY	1982
1374	LIVERPOOL	T42 DESTROYER	1982
1375	EDINBURGH	T42 DESTROYER	1985
1378	CAMPBELTOWN	T22 FRIGATE	1989
1379	UNSEEN	SUBMARINE	1991
1380	URSULA	SUBMARINE	1992
1381	UNICORN	SUBMARINE	1993

Epilogue
Margaret wants rid of shipbuilding.

1993 saw what was once known as Cammell Laird handover yet another submarine to the Royal Navy. HMS *Unicorn*, the last of four Upholder Class vessels, conventionally powered but exceptionally quiet running, vital in today's Navy, in which stealth is perceived as of greater importance than firepower.

But things change; the final irony for Cammell Laird was revealed only two weeks before the departure of HMS *Unicorn*. These submarines have been declared surplus to requirements in the latest defence review. They are to be sold off to the highest bidder. These submarines, brand spanking new, are still languishing in February 1998, on a remote dockside in Vickers yard in Barrow. They cost the British taxpayer, you and I, many millions of pounds.

The firepower for the British Navy of tomorrow is to be provided by four of the next generation of nuclear powered and nuclear-armed submarines. Trident.

These four vessels, the costs of which are almost impossible to estimate, are under construction at the VSEL shipyard in Barrow, Cammell Lairds' lead yard of the 1960s. In the heady days of denationalisation, when Lairds was swallowed up by it's 'Big Brother' the talk was of *'work sharing'*... *'a sensible decision given Lairds nuclear experience'* and the *'trickle down effect to Lairds of such a big contract'*.

It would be incorrect to say that Lairds had not had any of these promises kept. Some sections of Trident were fabricated at the Birkenhead yard. These have, however, been a 'cosmetic' sharing of the work. The reality was different. The 'parent' company wants all the work.

Lairds was the subject of some political jockeying for position and rhetoric. A 'Save our Shipyard' campaign was launched by the local press and pressure groups. A desperate search to find a buyer for the yard failed, or was hampered by the alleged 'hidden hands' of Vickers vetoing any deal. As one commentator stated ' if it floats, Lairds won't be building it.'

Recent statements by Mr (Sir) Brian Atkinson, former chairman of British Shipbuilders between 1980-1984 are now on public record stating that the when he presented his case to the government, in 1985, for the future of British Shipbuilding, he was told by an as yet unnamed very senior permanent government officer *'Brian,...... Margaret wants rid of shipbuilding.'*

The 'death warrant' for Cammell Laird was signed as early as 1985, in that most hallowed of all European political institutions, European Community Headquarters in Brussels, and neither Cammell Laird management nor workforce knew anything about it!

The Conservative government of the day led by Margaret Thatcher, accepted £140m in European aid and in return killed off nine British Shipbuilding yards, one of which was Cammell Laird in Birkenhead. Her chief hatchet man in this sacrificial demise, was, according to the same source, Mr. Norman Lamont, he of 'we have no intention of leaving the E.R.M'. fame. As my dad would have said, *'and the band played 'Believe it if you like'.*

When Cammell Laird was designated by the E.C. as a warship building yard in 1985, it was automatically denied access to the Shipbuilding Intervention Fund (S.I.F), a mechanism by which the shipbuilding industries of E.C. nations who were engaged upon the building of merchant ships could obtain subsidies upon their pricing policies.

The so called 'hidden agenda' of the time was the fact that their was no going back should the situation change, which, once again with hindsight for us mere mortals, it did; with the advent of the collapse of the Soviet Union and the resultant 'peace dividend.'

On July 5th 1985 Norman Lamont said of the S.I.F in a written answer to the House of Commons that... *'Aid of this kind ... will not normally be appropriate for, nor provided to, yards which have been or are about to be privatised by British Shipbuilders.'*

Sir Leon Britain, one time Conservative Chancellor, now 'spending more time with his family', is now on record as stating that *'if Cammell Lairds warship designation were to be changed ... the European Commission might ask for some of the aid back'.*

Perish the thought. He also stated that.... *'In 1985 the British Government undertook not to grant intervention fund aid to Cammell Laird in future as part of an overall reduction in capacity...... which was required as a counterpart to authorisation of a package of aid to British shipbuilders.'*

Cammell Lairds shipyard in Birkenhead has now closed. Mothballed for a while, but the 'smart money' is on redevelopment as a leisure centre/ theme park/ marina/ light industrial units of the kind that we are all too familiar with. Incredible as it may seem, investment grants will almost certainly be available to assist with any 'redevelopments'. Look out for *'Lairdside'*!

Cammell Laird had proven, over nearly two centuries, that they were more than capable of building the biggest and the best merchant ships, be they passenger liners or oil tankers. Why then were they denied the chance to fight it out in the world market using the same S.I.F that other 'Community" nations had access to?'........

The famous naval vessels that defended this country, the men that manned, and often died, on them apart;
The pioneering engineering spirit of this shipyards history apart;
The strikes and chequered industrial relations history of all shipbuilding yards in Britain apart;
The building of one half of Britain's then "necessary" nuclear deterrent apart;
The thousands of men who lost their jobs at Cammell Laird apart;
And perhaps saddest of all, those countless young people for whom the Cammell Lairds of this country will never again provide any real life training or skills apart.
The answer is as simple as it is, in my view, disgraceful.

Margaret wanted rid of shipbuilding.

David Roberts 1998